Fifty Years

Since MLK

Fifty Years

Since MLK

This issue of *Boston Review* is made possible by the generous support of THE FORD FOUNDATION and INCITE LABS

Editors-in-Chief Deborah Chasman, Joshua Cohen

Managing Editor Adam McGee

Senior Editor Chloe Fox

Web and Production Editor Avni Majithia-Sejpal

Poetry Editors Timothy Donnelly, BK Fischer, Stefania Heim

Fiction Editor Junot Díaz

Poetry Readers William Brewer, Julie Kantor, Becca Liu, Nick Narbutas, Diana Khoi Nguyen, Eleanor Sarasohn, Sean Zhuraw

Publisher Louisa Daniels Kearney

Marketing Manager Anne Boylan

Marketing Associate Michelle Betters

Finance Manager Anthony DeMusis III

Book Distributor The MIT Press, Cambridge, Massachusetts, and London, England

Magazine Distributor Disticor Magazine Distribution Services 800-668-7724, info@disticor.com

Printer Quad Graphics

Board of Advisors Derek Schrier (chairman), Archon Fung, Deborah Fung, Richard M. Locke, Jeff Mayersohn, Jennifer Moses, Scott Nielsen, Martha C. Nussbaum, Robert Pollin, Rob Reich, Hiram Samel, Kim Malone Scott

Cover and Graphic Design Zak Jensen

Typefaces Druk and Adobe Pro Caslon

Fifty Years Since MLK is *Boston Review* Forum 5 (43.1)

To become a member or subscribe, visit:
bostonreview.net/membership/

For questions about book sales or publicity, contact:
Michelle Betters, michelle@bostonreview.net

For questions about subscriptions, call 877-406-2443
or email Customer_Service@BostonReview.info.

Boston Review
PO Box 425786, Cambridge, MA 02142
617-324-1360

ISSN: 0734-2306 / ISBN: 978-1-946511-06-5

Editors' Note

FORUM

MLK Now

FORUM RESPONSES

Editors' Note

Deborah Chasman & Joshua Cohen

APRIL 4, 2018, marks the fiftieth anniversary of Martin Luther King, Jr.'s death. Once condemned by the head of the FBI as the "most notorious liar in the country," King is now widely celebrated as a national hero, a martyr to an inspiring dream about our country's largest possibilities.

In his lead article in this issue, Brandon M. Terry—political theorist and guest editor—underscores the costs of such canonization. In death King has come to be seen as an essentially conservative figure—a moralist who called Americans to keep faith with the country's exceptional values. No surprise then that "many younger Americans greet his name with suspicion."

We offer this issue as a corrective. Our contributors document and engage with King's profoundly radical political, moral, and religious thought. Instead of providing updated hagiographies, they show King in intellectual and political motion, learning from experience and struggle, moving from the fight against Jim Crow to the militarism and pervasive racial and economic injustice that were the country's "original sin."

While King's understanding of the deep roots of racial injustice will resonate powerfully with many activists today, other ideas may prove more challenging: King's ethical commitment to view political enemies as moral equals, his resistance to seeing racism as the cause of every racial disparity, his rejection of hate as an ethical stance, and his deep concern about the intrinsic importance of character and virtue.

Leading our forum, Terry looks closely at King's analysis of racism, his theorizing of collective action, and the role of virtue ethics in politics as King wrestled with strategies of civil disobedience and the implicit threat of violence. The responses and essays that follow work with King's ideas to consider the ethics of violent protest, the specter of racial capitalism, the possibilities for global solidarity, the limits of liberalism, the entanglement of race and foreign policy, and the possibility of structural reform.

King eventually worried that his increasingly radical call for a "revolution in values," one that would free human relationships from "systems of profit and governance," was a "fool's errand." But we abandon King's vision at our peril. We have much to learn both from his realistic picture of the depths of the problems we face and his inspiring hopes about the possibilities of achieving justice in all its forms.

King, as Terry reminds us, thought that Americans' "aversion to political radicalism remained an obstacle to critical thinking and good judgment." We are grateful the contributors here cast aside that aversion in service of the kind of critical thinking and good judgment that our country so desperately needs.

MLK Now

Brandon M. Terry

ON FEBRUARY 23, 1968, Martin Luther King, Jr., took to the stage at a sold-out Carnegie Hall. He had not come to rally the flagging spirits of bloodied civil rights demonstrators, shake loose the pennies of liberal philanthropists, or even to testify to God's grace. A more solemn task was at hand.

King was the keynote speaker for a centennial celebration of W. E. B. Du Bois's birth, following remarks by Ossie Davis, James Baldwin, Jack O'Dell, Cynthia Belgrave, Pete Seeger, and Eleanor McCoy. Arguably the greatest political thinker and propagandist black America ever produced, Du Bois spent his last days in relative ignominy in Ghana, his passport canceled by the U.S. State Department in retaliation for anti-nuclear, anti-racist, and socialist politics. Du Bois died on the eve of the 1963 March on Washington, denied the chance to witness the moral authority of the civil rights movement crystallize before the world.

In his address, King nevertheless urged that Du Bois's life—its "committed empathy with all the oppressed and . . . divine dissatisfaction with all forms of injustice"—had the pedagogical power "to teach us something about our tasks of emancipation." In King's judgment, Du Bois had combined the vocations of intellectual and organizer into "a single unified force" committed to the pursuit of justice, resisting both the temptations of wealth and renown that accrue to accommodationist politics, and the mystical authority and catharsis that give racial chauvinism its allure.

King also admonished those who denied that Du Bois—a founder of the National Association for the Advancement of Colored People (NAACP) in his youth and a member of the Communist Party in his twilight—was a "radical all of his life." Stating that Du Bois was "a genius and chose to be a Communist," King insinuated that Americans' reflexive aversion to political radicalism remained an obstacle to critical thinking and good judgment. Spoken barely forty days before King was shot dead on a Memphis motel balcony, the remarks honored Du Bois's trailblazing politics and, in hindsight, suggest worries King may have been harboring about his own legacy.

Those worries are easy to understand. In the year before King's death, he faced intense isolation owing to his strident criticisms of the Vietnam War and the Democratic Party, his heated debates with black nationalists, and his headlong quest to mobilize the nation's poor against economic injustice. Abandoned by allies, fearing his death was near, King could only lament that his critics "have never really known me, my commitment, or my calling."

Fifty years after his death, we are perhaps subject to the same indictment. As we grasp for a proper accounting of King's intellectual, ethical, and political bequest, commemoration may present a greater obstacle to an honest reckoning with his legacy than disfavor did in the case of Du Bois. There are costs to canonization.

Terry

The King now enshrined in popular sensibilities is not the King who spoke so powerfully and admiringly at Carnegie Hall about Du Bois. Instead, he is a mythic figure of consensus and conciliation, who sacrificed his life to defeat Jim Crow and place the United States on a path toward a "more perfect union." In this familiar view, King and the civil rights movement are rendered—as Cass Sunstein approvingly put it—"backward looking and even conservative." King deployed his rhetorical genius in the service of our country's deepest ideals—the ostensible consensus at the heart of our civic culture—and dramatized how Jim Crow racism violated these commitments. Heroically, through both word and deed, he called us to be true to who we *already* are: "to live out the true meaning" of our founding creed. No surprise, then, that King is often draped in Christian symbolism redolent of these themes. He is a revered prophet of U.S. progress and redemption, Moses leading the Israelites to the Promised Land, or a Christ who sacrificed his life to redeem our nation from its original sin.

Such poetic renderings lead our political and moral judgment astray. Along with the conservative gaslighting that claims King's authority for "colorblind" jurisprudence, they obscure King's persistent attempt to jar the United States out of its complacency and corruption. They ignore his indictment of the United States as the "greatest purveyor of violence in the world," his critique of a Constitution unjustly inattentive to economic rights and racial redress, and his condemnation of municipal boundaries that foster unfairness in housing and schooling. It is no wonder then that King's work is rarely on the reading lists of young activists. He has become an icon to quote, not a thinker and public philosopher to engage.

This is a tragedy, for King was a vital political thinker. Unadulterated, his ideas upset convention and pose radical challenges—perhaps especially today, amidst a gathering storm of authoritarianism, racial chauvinism, and nihilism that threatens the future of democracy and the ideal of equality. What follows is an effort to recover those unsettling ideas by shedding light on three of the most important and misunderstood elements of King's mature thought: his analysis of racism; his political theory of direct action and civil disobedience; and his understanding of the place of ethical virtues in activism and social life.

IN KING'S WORK, the point of philosophical reflection on racism is *political*: "the prescription for the cure rests with the accurate diagnosis of the disease." Having the right theoretical understanding of racism—one of the "triple evils" of the United States, along with militarism and poverty—is, in other words, a critical element of effective activism.

King's theory of racism has three main components. First, drawing on the insights of E. Franklin Frazier, King argued that racism is deeply entangled with "irrational fears"—of losing economic or social standing, of contamination, of an unknown future, and, above all, of revenge and retaliation. The desire to escape or sublimate this fear, King reasoned, generates "strange psychoses and peculiar cases of paranoia." This account of the affective dimension of racism—especially its entwinement with terror—sharply diverges from models which contend that rational argumentation or moral suasion are sufficient tools to undermine racism.

The second element in King's understanding of racism is sociopolitical. King insisted that "it is necessary to refute the idea that the dominant ideology in our country even today is freedom and equality while racism is just an occasional departure from the norm on the part of a few bigoted extremists." Instead, King rightly argued, the persistence of racial domination, and the resilience of white racial resentment, "lies in the 'congenital deformity' of racism that has crippled the nation from its inception." Yet, in King's mapping of U.S. political history, "the democratic spirit that has always faced [racism] is equally real" and remains a source of hope and wisdom. King's unapologetic identification with this democratic spirit throws down a gauntlet of sorts. It still divides, as it did then, those who see the struggle for racial democracy as a series of exemplary strivings, partial victories, and genuine missed opportunities from those who see the U.S. racial order as originary and permanent, making every revolt, cynical or heroic, always already a gesture of futility.

The third element of King's understanding of racism is that it arises from cognitive and empathetic failures. The practices we associate with racism—segregation, discrimination, exploitation, political subordination, and even genocide—all, on King's account, express a "contempt for life." Indulging "the arrogant assertion that one race is the center of value," racism cultivates a habitual blindness to our fellows' capacities and even existence. Channeling Du Bois, King links this to an arrogance that precludes racists from believing stigmatized groups have contributed to "the progress of history" or "can assure the progress of the future." As a practical matter, then, uprooting racial injustice entails critiquing its legitimating ideas. This means targeting the stereotypes, narratives, and stigmas that underpin racial domination, especially ones that espouse "passivity" as a justification.

"The nation," King lamented in *Why We Can't Wait* (1964), "had come to count on [the Negro] as a creature who could quietly endure, silently suffer and patiently wait." It was, he insisted, only the spectacle of mass, disciplined, direct action that finally "dissolved the stereotype of the grinning, submissive Uncle Tom" and forced the country to see ordinary African Americans as "active organ[s] of change." While historians of African American politics have excavated the long history of struggle that belies the myth of black passivity, King was right to admit that enduring domination also extracts real submission. What mass protest enacts, on King's account, is the transformation of blacks' own self-respect, as well as a forceful push for the broader public to recognize blacks as co-creators of a democratic society.

What is especially critical about King's understanding of racism is the synergy of these three components. Debates about racism tend to either get mired in the search for intentional discrimination and malicious prejudice, or drawn into an all-too-easy equation of racial disparity with "institutional" racism or "white supremacy." King, by contrast, tried to be precise about the various causes of black disadvantage while fashioning a conception of racism attentive to its multifaceted power and formative influence.

For example, if we downplay the role that irrational fears play in racism, we often leap abruptly to charges of intentional discrimination and ill will, and thus a consequent desire to punish racists. This fuels the mob mentality, virtue signaling, and scapegoating that dominate much of what passes now for discourse on racial justice. Or if we treat racism primarily as a question of ignorance without taking its intellectual content seriously, the cure becomes "consciousness-raising," a didactic, hierarchical, educative politics to reform the souls of fellow citizens. In its professional variant, this paradigm proliferates as "diversity" training; in its protest strain, it is defended as having "started a conversation," regardless of whether such politics are persuasive or polarizing.

Likewise, if we ignore the sociopolitical dimension, we may treat racism as near-immutable and overstate its explanatory effects. In treating anti-blackness, in Ta-Nehisi Coates's words, as "a force of nature," one of "our world's physical laws," it can become easy to lose track of the historical and present-day contingencies of race and racial hierarchy. The weight of the past, enormous as it is, must be an aid, not an obstacle, to understanding new features of our racial order. In addition to engaging questions of political economy and gender ideology, thinking about race today means grasping phenomena such as the unprecedented class differentiation among the African American population; the role

Islamophobia, nativism, and anti-Latino attitudes play in U.S. politics; the opioid epidemic and life-expectancy decline among white Americans; and how the movement of Asian American men into the top income bracket has become a central concern of right-wing nativism and nationalism. A lack of precision impairs our ability to draw perceptive moral distinctions between different ills and injustices by treating everything—from Hollywood awards and university syllabi to police violence and mass shootings—as all part of a white supremacist totality, which finds full and complete expression in every social phenomenon.

For racial pessimists, the options are even worse. Hope itself becomes a foolish compulsion. Philosopher Calvin Warren, for example, argues that King's nonviolent politics and ethic of sacrifice offer only "the humiliated, incarcerated, mutilated, and terrorized black body" as the "vestibule" for a democracy that will never come. In the face of this despair, pessimists console themselves with fugitive gestures of dissent and denunciation. Their view of racism is often so profoundly total that they cast black life in late capitalism as intrinsically heroic—whether it takes the form of burdened endurance among the black poor, the mundane "self-care" indulgences of black elites, or the self-professed nihilism of black cultural critics.

Finally, if we ignore the cognitive dimensions of racism, we miss King's contention, in *Where Do We Go from Here* (1967), that "the value in pulling racism out of its obscurity and stripping it of its rationalizations lies in the confidence that it can be changed." We also fail to grasp the nature of his faith in political resistance, or the scale at which it aims. In "The Dangerous Road Before Martin Luther King" (1961), James Baldwin lauded King as the first "black leader" able "to carry the battle [over racial injustice] into the individual heart and make its resolution the province of the individual will." This misunderstands King, however, who seemed less interested in the "racism of the individual heart" than in unmasking the *ideas* of black inferiority that served to rationalize oppression. King's interests in fear, ideology, and politics led him to believe, as he expressed in "The Power of Nonviolence" (1958), that we must "attack the evil system rather than individuals who happen to be caught up in the system."

This systemic focus, crucially, does not inflate "racism" to make it explain *all* racial disparities, but understands that such inequalities are outcomes of many phenomena that interact with racism, *yet cannot be reduced to* only racism. These include technology, political economy, and cultural patterns. As early as 1964, for example, King presciently warned in *Why We Can't Wait* that "if automation is a threat to Negroes, it is equally a menace to organized labor." Arguing for an alliance between civil rights and labor activists, King foresaw how capital investments in "efficiency" would dislocate middle-class jobs, stagnate wages, and devastate unions' political power. Granted, discrimination and historical disadvantage would cause these burdens to fall *hardest* on poor blacks—yet it still opened the possibility of broader political alliances. Indeed, part of what made King worry in *Where Do We Go From Here* that black nationalism was a dead end was that it seemed to give "priority to race precisely at a time when the impact of automation and other forces have made the economic question fundamental for blacks and whites alike."

IN KING'S RECOUNTING in *Why We Can't Wait* and *Where Do We Go From Here*, the history of black politics included several crucial "discoveries," such as the black nationalist turn toward black pride, or the litigation strategies of the NAACP. Despite these leaps forward, however, King saw the black political tradition as historically stuck in "dead ends" of accommodationist conservatism, elitism, separatism, and legal fetishism. What had allowed black politics to finally escape these doldrums, according to King, was the adoption and refinement of Gandhian nonviolent direct action and civil disobedience. Judging nonviolent resistance to be the "only morally and practically sound method open to oppressed people in their struggle for freedom," as he described it in *Stride Toward Freedom* (1957), King came to appreciate its unique power to undermine racial domination and revitalize democratic politics from below.

Perhaps because of the outsized influence of his 1963 "Letter from a Birmingham Jail," we tend to think of King's embrace of civil disobedience as a moral refusal to obey unjust laws that do not conform to higher, natural law. Rarely, however, does civil disobedience manifest this exceptional congruence—nor should it need to. While Rosa Parks, student sit-ins, and Freedom Riders all transgressed particular laws or policies they hoped to overturn, it was more often the case that civil rights activists merely transgressed laws of public order. Thus, as King argued in front of the New York Bar Association in 1965, the justification of civil disobedience is not that it specifically targets an unjust law, but that it is a goad, "call[ing] attention to overall injustice" in communities that "do not work with vigor and with determination to remove that injustice."

This is among the reasons why King, unlike many liberals of his generation (including John Rawls and later Bayard Rustin), was adamant that civil disobedience should be used to attack unjust economic inequalities as well as civil rights violations and conscription. Lacking faith that rights protections, union politics, and formal political participation were sufficient tools to spur economic justice (especially after the disappointments of the Johnson administration), King worried in *Why We Can't Wait* that, without mass action, the poor would be left "on a lonely island of economic insecurity in the midst of a vast ocean of material prosperity." In the face of accelerating automation and the elimination of living-wage jobs, King endorsed a number of egalitarian policies, including basic income and a full-employment guarantee, which have once again become rallying cries. Our present-day interest in these policies, however, remains too tethered to technocratic governance. King thought only mass civil disobedience would create, shape, and sustain such transformative goals.

King's vision for civil disobedience cannot be separated from his concern with the "evil" of poverty. King argued that our species needs to undergo a dramatic ethical shift in how we think about our relationship to resources, now that we no longer face scarcity. "The contemporary tendency," King protested in *Where Do We Go From Here*, "is to base our distribution on scarcity, which has vanished, and to compress our abundance into the overfed mouths of the middle and upper classes until they gag with superfluity." As he wrote in *Strength to Love* (1963), to countenance "a gulf between superfluous wealth and abject poverty," or "take necessities from the many to give luxuries to the few," is to cultivate a citizenry of the "cold and conscienceless." Near the end of his life, King hoped in *The Trumpet of Conscience* (1968) that the "Negro revolt" would rescue democracy from this "archaic" cruelty by evolving into a full-fledged "challenge to a system that has created miracles of production and technology" but had left many of scarcity's habits and hierarchies intact. For King, such persistent failures of reciprocity— political, social, and economic—made civil disobedience legitimate.

To be sure, civil disobedience raises questions beyond moral legitimacy. For King, civil disobedience and other forms of nonviolent direct action possess substantial political and ethical merits as well. They are needed to "supplement" procedural liberalism, resisting domination directly. Moreover, unlike the elite politics of lobbying, legislation, and litigation that preoccupied the midcentury NAACP, or the masculinist insurrection that briefly attracted the interest of Frantz Fanon's self-proclaimed disciples on the left, King noted in *Why We Can't Wait* that "a nonviolent army has a magnificent universal quality." It can transcend many of the kinds of exclusion that other forms of political action place on participation, including those of gender, age, physical disability, education, and wealth. The mass dimension of protest allows for people of all walks of life to be more than spectators, and instead be transformed by their resistance to oppression, rediscovering courage and self-respect in the face of assaults on their dignity.

Indeed, King's understanding of structural injustice—and the importance of mass participation as a coercive countervailing force—goes a long way toward explaining his radicalization over time. Early in his career, King's case for nonviolent protest turned primarily on its capacity to elicit shame and spiritual conversion. By 1963 in Birmingham, however, faced with the massive resistance of segregationists (manipulative court injunctions and evasive legal maneuvers, police brutality, surveillance, and outright terrorism), King began to embrace the coercive and realist dimensions of nonviolent direct action. "The purpose of our direct-action program," he proclaimed in "Letter from a Birmingham Jail," "is to create a situation so crisis-packed that it will inevitably open the door to negotiation."

King's admission of the *coercive* dimension of civil disobedience raises serious ethical quandaries about the exercise of such power. When should civil disobedients break the law? Or boycotts cripple a business? Or public space and public goods be occupied using intimidation? The hagiography around the civil rights movement has allowed Americans to mostly evade such questions, but the sublime and disruptive force of mass civil disobedience is still apparent wherever it topples a government overseas or invites police surveillance and suppression at home.

King, to his credit, was acutely aware of this and devoted enormous attention to theorizing the ways direct action could be ethically organized and sustained. Combining moral commitments with considerations of political efficacy, King thought that direct action needed to be disciplined and channeled through ideals of nonviolence and public appeal, love and sacrifice, integration and democracy. In our more secular and pluralist era, however, the roots of King's thinking in a knotty metaphysics of natural law and Christian ethics may invite suspicion. Indeed, given the ample historical record of unrequited love, unredeemed sacrifice, and failed integration, it is easily argued that such sacrifices are not just beyond the duties of the disadvantaged but indeed masochistic.

Yet we should not allow this suspicion of religion, or our era's narrow focus on duty at the expense of other ethical categories, to narrow our concerns. As philosopher Tommie Shelby has argued, drawing on Rawls, invocations of civic duty first require a serious confrontation with the unfairness of the basic structure of society. Moreover, ethical reflection does not simply concern duties and fairness. We must contend as well with the good, the virtuous, and the heroic. King's example teaches this, while also demonstrating that ethical judgments and convictions are strengthened, rather than diluted, by clear-eyed realism.

However, King's realism is easily misunderstood. His defenses of civil disobedience, particularly in his early career, are replete with exhortations to take on unearned suffering and voluntary sacrifice in order to win the "friendship and understanding" of one's opponents. Psychologist Kenneth Clark, whose testimony played a key role in *Brown v. Board of Education* (1954), told King that he felt it was "too much" to expect that "a group of human beings who have been the victims of cruelty and flagrant injustice could actually love those who have been associated with the perpetrators, if not the perpetrators themselves." For Malcolm X, King's brotherly rhetoric was simply disingenuous because King actually *relied* upon the threat of violent rebellion from below. It was only when "Negroes took to the streets" in the Birmingham riots following the bombing of King's brother's house, Malcolm proclaimed in "Message to the Grass Roots" (1963), that "Kennedy sent in the troops . . . [and] put out a civil-rights bill."

Terry

These are still challenging contentions. If the threat of violence from below is part of what draws Americans' attention to protest, from Birmingham to Ferguson, what kind of "nonviolence" does this amount to? How should we, in our own time, account for the fact that the cameras disappeared in Missouri when the threat of violent rebellion subsided? Or, likewise, that Ferguson remains far more well known than the reliably peaceful Moral Mondays movement, in which protestors assembled at the North Carolina state legislature weekly for over a year (2013–14) to be arrested in protest of conservatives' assaults on voting rights, civil liberties, and social welfare?

Yet, for King, despite disobedience's complicated relationship with coercion, its nonviolent aspect remained crucial, in part because of its unique ability to throw racist ideology off balance. On King's account, the racist worldview predicts that the humiliation and disregard dispensed in its name will bring back more of the same. Thus, the longstanding obsession —from Thomas Jefferson to Steve Bannon—with the possible revenge of the world of color against the white world. This fear of anti-white reprisal inspires not only *backlash*, but *preemptive* suppression—what Vesla Weaver has called "frontlash." For King, "adherence to nonviolence—which also means *love* in its strong and commanding sense," politically performed a feat of redirection. By unsettling racist expectations and disclosing new possibilities for living together, nonviolence and an ethic of love became vehicles for staging grievance, disrupting distrust and retaliation, and envisioning new forms of cooperation.

This concept of love—which King referred to as *agape*, to distinguish it from erotic or romantic love—builds on an ethics distilled from the Parable of the Good Samaritan and Jesus' commandment to "love thy neighbor as thyself." King's defense of love in contentious politics enjoins us to see even our political *enemies* as moral equals whom we are interdependent with and vulnerable to, and whose needs and welfare we are obligated to consider. We deform the richness of human sociability, King insists, if we allow particularity, enmity, and anger to blind us to this.

While granting the legitimacy of black rage, King argued that it was best, both politically and for one's own flourishing, to channel anger into less corrosive emotions. Above all, one must avoid the slippage of anger into hatred, a disposition which "destroys a man's sense of values and his objectivity." Hatred blankets the world with suspicion, smothering our broad capacities for appreciation, analysis, and responsiveness. As King warned, it can lead us "to describe the beautiful as ugly and the ugly as beautiful, and to confuse the true with the false and the false with the true."

For King, one of the great lessons of Du Bois's life was that "he did not content himself with hurling invectives for emotional release and then to retire into smug, passive satisfaction." "It is not enough for people to be angry," King argued; "the supreme task is to organize and unite people so that their anger becomes a transforming force." Crucially, King never denied the existence of righteous anger or the threat of rebellion, but incorporated these passions into his political thinking as challenges to be redirected toward worthier ends.

One concrete implication of this view—beyond curbing the impulse to mock and condemn on social media—is to avoid forms of political resistance that seek to "humiliate the opponent" rather than "win his friendship and understanding." These vengeful approaches deny others the capacities for moral learning. They foreclose unanticipated forms of reconciliation and community, and judge, a priori, the life horizons of others based on their worst transgressions, cognitive mistakes, or group identities. Worse, the misguided notion that such practices build partisan solidarity and affirmation are woefully shortsighted. Inevitably, such passions turn inward, destroying organizations with recrimination, excommunications, and cynicism.

Importantly, however, King's demand cuts in two directions. His faith in redemptive possibility precludes embittered disengagement and spiteful retaliation, *but does not license complacency.* It instead demands unyielding confrontation in pursuit of the greater goods of a more just world. To exhort us to the former without insisting on the latter—as many critics of the left continue to do—is to settle for "a negative peace which is the absence of tension" rather than "a positive peace which is the presence of justice."

IN THE DECADES following his death, cynical appropriations of King have become such a reliable feature of public discourse that many younger Americans greet his name with suspicion. Indeed, even those in the Movement for Black Lives, despite commitments to nonviolent direct action and democratic politics, have often sought ostensibly more "radical" ancestors to claim, such as Malcolm X, Assata Shakur, Fred Hampton, and Audre Lorde.

Perhaps this is penance that had to be paid. King's blindness to the gendered dimensions of charismatic authority and hierarchical leadership within protest organizations—and the black church—is surely reason enough to be critical of his example. And, as Shatema Threadcraft and I have written at length elsewhere, while King became intensely supportive of women-led welfare and tenants' unions, heralded the inclusive quality of civil disobedience, and promoted the guaranteed-income policy foundational to left feminism, his essentialist views on gender and normative views on the family suffer from severe logical and moral failures. This is the most glaring weakness in King's thought and the piece that, rightly, has received the most thorough contemporary critique. Any retrieval of King's legacy has to amend his triple evils to include a fourth: sexism.

Moreover, the black church—which in the nineteenth century Martin Delany called the "Alpha and Omega" in black communities—is today a profoundly weakened institution. The church faces many challenges in our era of political and social integration, prosperity theology, political party clientelism, social conservatism, and heavily publicized sexual and financial corruption. King's theological commitments were once part of his allure. Now they present an impediment to his embrace among the "unchurched." One wonders whether the Christian roots of King's political and ethical vision, and the incredible tradition of church-based organizing that brought it to life, can be suitably rethought in other institutions and traditions, or revived at all in its home.

Some of the present eschewal of King, however, seems less fair and more superficial. In a world irrevocably transformed by the sexual revolution and secularism—not to mention urbanity, black street culture, and the ascendancy of ironic art and self-expression—King can appear both terribly staid and uncomfortably earnest. Burdened with utterly unique political responsibility and his own impossible standards of ethical excellence, King's words and persona seem weighed down, even beyond the grave, with a self-restraint that can make him feel older, less "cool," and more distant than black male contemporaries such as Malcolm X or Baldwin.

These qualities lead some to associate King with what has come to be called "respectability politics." Such critics fail to note, though, that historian Evelyn Brooks Higginbotham introduced the concept to mark out a *dual* concern among black activists. The first kind of respectability politics, the version that young activists rightly skewer, is concerned with undermining, through personal conduct, stereotypes about blacks' deviance from social norms of public comportment, sexual mores, and socioeconomic achievement. This politics is justified only insofar as it works, and, consequently, contemporary debates quickly degenerate into competing judgments of efficacy and how to weigh the worth against the indignity of supplicative appeals to white sufferance.

King can fairly be criticized for not fully interrogating, for example, why Montgomery was able to summon enthusiastic solidarity for Rosa Parks but not for less "reputable" victims of Jim Crow. But he never entertained the indefensible respectability-politics proposition that blacks must "prove" themselves fit for equal *citizenship*. Even early in his career, when often writing of the need for blacks to improve personal standards, King criticized the cruelty and irrationality of the ostracism and economic burdens visited upon unmarried parents and the incarcerated. Later, King would declare ghetto crime to be "derivative" of "the greater crimes of white society" in housing, policing, employment, and education. And it is absurd to ascribe to King—a prominent defender of a coercive, confrontational politics of civil disobedience with a sophisticated theory of racism—the anodyne view that "respectable" personal conduct would ever be sufficient to cripple racist ideology.

That said, King did articulate strong convictions about certain standards of personal conduct and comportment. But the justifications he offered were more in line with Higginbotham's *second* version of a politics of respectability: the age-old concern with the social bases of ethical virtues. King's interest in compassion, humility, generosity, courage, thrift, and magnanimity was animated by the judgment that these virtues are essential to one's own dignity and self-respect, and ultimately to the *goodness* of one's life. Perhaps better described as a politics of *character*, King's standards of personal excellence; his warnings against anger, racial chauvinism, and bitterness; and his overriding emphasis on nonviolence and love are part of this ethical tradition.

If oppression sabotages the oppressed's strivings to live well mainly through a subtle, pernicious evil that suffuses daily life, then the struggle to cultivate and sustain ethical virtues becomes its own battlefront. To ignore that emancipatory struggle demands certain virtues, or to deny that these virtues have significance for the good life, is self-defeating. Even more ignoble is to present such virtues of character as efforts to imitate whites—thus equating whiteness with virtue and flattering perhaps the silliest, most self-deluded and analytically bankrupt conceit of white supremacy.

Now, one may insist (implausibly, I think) that rage is not corrosive to our judgments of beauty and truth, or of the good and the right. Or one may assail the conception of human flourishing on which rests King's claims about personal standards (his approach to gender would be a great place to start). One may even reject particular virtues, such as humility or magnanimity, as originating in false consciousness or ressentiment. But these concerns at least engage with King as a serious thinker, rather than reduce these commitments to a certain kind of respectability.

Developing a richer understanding of King's commitments helps us to better appreciate his *departures* from conventional markers of respectability, including his qualified support of hippie pacifism as well as his celebration of black student protestors who "threw off their middle-class values" and ceased imitating whites in "dress, conduct and thought." It also helps us grasp why, when King spent much of 1966 in Chicago's slums attempting to galvanize a protest movement against ghettoization, he sought to organize gang members, to the consternation of many. Transgressing the norms of a Southern Baptist preacher, King recruited gang affiliates in pool halls and on street corners, and even invited them into his home, engaging them in long debates and training them in nonviolent methods. Such efforts, which have been obscured in King's legacy, sit provocatively alongside the work of the Black Panthers and Nation of Islam, and anticipate efforts of present-day organizers in Baltimore, St. Louis, and elsewhere.

ENGAGING KING'S IDEAS about racism, political action, and ethics is, of course, not the same as agreeing with him, much less treating him as the object of uncritical adulation. It is simply to treat him as a profound interlocutor

Terry

and model of political judgment. King teaches us that the morphology of protest should be treated as a perpetual question, one experimentally and imaginatively rethought in light of technological, cultural, political changes.

This learning will not be easy. Our saturation with images of suffering (black and otherwise) and the balkanization of the media have altered how we respond to documentary images, raising doubts about whether we remain as receptive to King's strategies of public spectacle. Racial stereotypes have also transformed. Few would now identify blacks with passivity; on the contrary, black protestors are regularly labeled as aggressive, ungrateful, and dangerous. Social media has created a low-cost outlet for every utterance of resentment to gain a hearing. The practice of public assembly has been forever altered by the possibility of terrorism. And nonviolent resistance has become ritualized, with police trained in forms of protest management that rob civil disobedience of the drama of punishment and sacrifice that once gave it gravitas. Street marches, as King predicted, now need to reach massive levels of participation and organization if they are not to be "mere transitory drama" absorbed by "the normal turbulence of city life."

Even the geopolitics of protest has changed. Authoritarian rulers are ascendant at home and abroad, European liberals are in retreat, and Donald Trump (as Barack Obama did before him) issues unilateral, global assassination orders from an office decorated with King's bust. The idea that Americans will be ashamed in the eyes of the world, central to King's Cold War–era politics, now seems quaint. In recognition of this shift, the longstanding interest among black activists in symbolic appeals to the United Nations and human rights forums has been eclipsed by a mix of domestic protest and electoral politics.

Still King's call to internationalize nonviolent social justice movements continues to matter in at least one important respect. We face global existential challenges of climate change, nuclear weaponry, war and terrorism, and wealth inequality (abetted by offshore tax havens and attacks on capital controls). Yet the institutions that exercise the most power over these circumstances remain insulated from democratic action and accountability to citizens. If there is any hope to prevent disempowered citizens' rage and resentment from being exploited by demagogues and reactionaries, it must be channeled into coordinated, enduring social movements that force electoral and economic reckonings while fostering respect for our shared "garment of destiny."

King was hopeful, but not blind to the difficulty and costs of these aspirations. Members of such movements will face repression, scorn, prison, and sacrifice. Racism and sexism will threaten solidarity, violence will injure our faith in cooperation, and inequality will breed its rationalizations. But when threats are mortal, retreat and accommodation are avenues to self-destruction. As we scour for exemplars of struggle, we must not write off the United States' most peculiar radical and his enduring intellectual and political challenge. King calls on us to think and argue publicly about the crises of our present, and collectively determine the broadest range of nonviolent coercive powers at our disposal. "Our very survival," King wrote in *Where Do We Go From Here*, "depends on our ability to stay awake, to adjust to new ideas, to remain vigilant and to face the challenge of change." The spirit of King is most alive when we embrace these challenges and endeavor, with courage, humility, and a sense of the great sacrifices ahead, to shape a new world out of divine dissatisfaction with injustice.

Terry

King in Context

Barbara Ransby

BRANDON TERRY'S ESSAY reminds me of the words of the late Vincent Harding, Martin Luther King, Jr.'s close friend: "Dead men make such convenient heroes." It is a warning to those who would praise King not to fall prey to selective amnesia and sanitize him in ways that distort his legacy.

In response to Terry's thoughtful essay, I would like, first, to further contextualize King, socially and historically; second, to foreground the class politics embedded in who we remember and how; and third, to revisit the politics of respectability in light of today's Movement for Black Lives.

IN REMEMBERING and re-engaging King, we must be attentive to his historical context and the people who surrounded him. King was not a solitary political actor, and his ideas were not his alone; they were a product of interactions with a wide and vibrant set of people and events that inspired, challenged, and altered his thinking. As Ella Baker put it, Martin did not make the movement, the movement made Martin.

Notably, fierce and formidable women were as much a part of shaping King's worldview as anyone else. Chief among them was Coretta Scott King, a civil rights activist before she met King and a strong advocate for civil and human rights long after his death; she took a strong stance on LGBTQ issues when many of her generation remained silent. Other women who influenced King included Baker, a veteran activist and proponent of grassroots leadership; Dorothy Cotton, a dynamic strategist, organizer, and adviser; and Diane Nash, leader of the Student Nonviolent Coordinating Committee who later worked with King's Southern Christian Leadership Conference, bringing her radical democratic sensibilities with her.

In addition to the influence of the women around King, we should also consider the poor and working-class people who surrounded King in the final years of his life, when he turned his attention to planning for the Poor People's Campaign and speaking out against U.S. imperialism and capitalism. Terry begins his essay with a lesser-known King speech, delivered on February 23, 1968, in honor of W. E. B. Du Bois. I suggest we start a couple weeks earlier, on February 1, 1968.

On that rainy day in Memphis, two poor, black sanitation workers—35-year-old Echol Cole and 29-year-old Robert Walker—were riding in the back of a garbage truck when its faulty grinding mechanism malfunctioned. They were crushed, suffering painful, gruesome deaths. Walker's young wife was pregnant at the time. The men earned 500 dollars a month, had no benefits or life insurance, and both families struggled to afford the burial costs. The deaths of Cole and Walker triggered a 64-day strike of 1,300 black sanitation workers in Memphis. King went there to lend support.

So, in recalibrating the legacy of King, we have to include men such as Cole and Walker. They too are martyrs of a different type, casualties of racial capitalism and the ravages of poverty and racism, the evils that King was so determined to combat, along with militarism.

UNDERSTANDING KING'S class context is especially important when analyzing his stance on the politics of respectability, and equally so for appreciating why the Movement for Black Lives rejects respectability politics. Terry asks us to reconsider a very particular meaning of the term that historian Evelyn Brooks Higginbotham had in mind when she coined it in 1993. However, here, too, context matters.

During the civil rights movement's nonviolent sit-ins and boycotts, protesters presented a clean-cut image to garner national sympathy for the struggle. Low-wage workers, however, who lacked formal education, status, or title—men such as Cole and Walker—often could not or would not conform to the protocols of respectable behavior and comportment dictated by the middle class. To follow the rules in some cases meant to swallow their righteous anger. To dress and speak according to certain middle-class norms was to distance themselves from the communities that nurtured them. The exclusionary politics of respectability often put them outside the bounds of protected citizens or sympathetic victims. And patterns of protest did too. The Memphis struggle included militant rebellion by the city's poor and working class, as well as orderly marches.

To his credit, King wrestled with the contradictions of preaching nonviolence to poor, angry young people forced to live in a violent world. In his famous "Beyond Vietnam" speech of 1967, King confessed: "I knew that I could never again raise my voice against the violence of the oppressed in the ghettos without having first spoken clearly to the greatest purveyor of violence in the world today—my own government."

As Michelle Alexander argues, building on the work of prison abolitionists such as Ruthie Gilmore and Angela Davis, many poor black people who have been disproportionately victimized and villainized by the carceral state have been reduced to a permanent marginalized

Ransby

caste in our society. If you are a felon or a formerly incarcerated person (overwhelmingly poor and working-class people of color), you are socially exiled from "respectable" circles: excluded from voting, from certain professions, subject to added surveillance and housing and employment discrimination. If you are a woman, your sexual past and present practices also determine your status. And if you are queer, it is an uphill climb to be included under any circumstances. Yet these three groups—poor black people, women, and queer people—have been at the forefront of today's Black Freedom struggle against state violence.

During the uprisings in Ferguson and Baltimore in 2014 and 2015, reporters and pundits often drew a line of demarcation between the "good" protesters, those who knelt in prayer, followed the rules, and went home before curfew; and the "bad" protesters, who broke windows, refused to disperse, and used profanity to describe the profane police violence. The latter group was in the streets the longest, refusing to back down, defying authority, and confronting the defenders of the status quo. These are the irreverent and implacable young people to whom Barack Obama preached calm and whom Bill Cosby mocked and maligned.

Embracing a black feminist praxis, this generation's Black Freedom leaders have rejected the politics of respectability. They insist that the voices of black queer organizers be heard loud and clear, and that assertive women be honored within the movement. Rather than eschewing the marginalized and often maligned sectors of the community, the Movement for Black Lives' organizers have prioritized them: arguing that those who suffer most from the policies of racial capitalism ought to be at the center of an agenda for racial justice.

For the most part, today's movement has rejected a top-down, charismatic, male-centered model of leadership. But it has not forgotten King as much as Terry fears. In 2016 and 2017, the Movement for Black Lives marked the King holiday by calling on activists to remember the radical King, the internationalist King. In dozens of cities, local groups held vigils, teach-ins, marches, and rallies with that theme in mind.

Fifty years after King's assassination, the most important corrective we can make, Terry rightly suggests, is to take King down from the pedestal. It is too narrow, too high, and too confining. And it distances King from the people and struggles that helped to define him.

The Pivot to Class

Keeanga-Yamahtta Taylor

IN A POSTHUMOUSLY published essay, Martin Luther King, Jr., pointed out that the "black revolution" had gone beyond the "rights of Negroes." The struggle, he said, is "forcing America to face all of its interrelated flaws—racism, poverty, militarism and materialism. It is exposing the evils that are rooted deeply in the whole structure of our society. It reveals systemic rather than superficial flaws and suggests that radical reconstruction of society itself is the real issue to be faced."

But it had not started out that way. Over the course of a decade, the black struggle opened up a deeper interrogation of U.S. society, and King's politics traversed the same course.

Indeed, in the early 1960s, the southern movement coalesced around the clearly defined demands to end Jim Crow segregation and secure the right of African Americans to unfettered access to the franchise. With clear targets and barometers for progress or failure, a broad social movement was able to uproot these systems of oppression. King was lauded as a tactician as well as someone who could articulate the grievances and aspirations of black southerners.

But despite the successful example of nonviolent civil disobedience across the South, it appeared to have little, if any, lasting impact on the edifice of racial discrimination that defined black life elsewhere. Indeed, the seeming permanence of black marginalization across the United States produced hundreds of urban uprisings in the middle of the 1960s. If King's strategic genius in the South was deploying nonviolent civil disobedience to disarm southern racists while *coercing* the political establishment into securing first-class citizen rights, it was a strategy that ultimately failed in cities such as Los Angeles, Chicago, Philadelphia, and Washington, D.C. In those places, obnoxious signs of Jim Crow were not the problem; rather, it was the insidious but obscured actions of the real estate broker, the banker, the employer, the police officer, and other agents that maintained racial inequality.

As King's attention drifted from the South to the entrenched northern ghettos, he faced denunciations and chastisement from former allies in the North. These people had supported him so long as he confined his demands to ending legal discrimination. Indeed, because southern racism was rendered as antiquated and regressive, King was celebrated for helping to pull the South toward progress and modernity. But even as the civil rights movement was valorized for its intervention in the South, it was demonized when it brought its call for black power and liberation to the North—a dynamic that continues to the present day.

In King's time, institutions in the North that preached racial neutrality but that were wholly complicit in racial subjugation appeared impervious to tactics that used confrontation and embarrassment to compel change. King was forced to reconceive his strategy.

King's confrontation with Chicago mayor Richard J. Daley, for instance, was instructive. When King went to Chicago in 1966 to participate in an ongoing campaign to end slums in the city's black West Side, he was confronted by the obstinacy of patronage-fueled machine politics. African American gatekeepers viewed King as an interloper, and the mayor viewed him as a nuisance. Daley simply denied that there was a ghetto in Chicago, and the black political machine exhorted that the ghetto's existence was proof positive of racial progress. They deprived King of the spectacle of confrontation that had exposed the southern establishment.

It was this foray into the tough political environment of residential segregation and political machines that provided the momentum for King's radicalization. His political maturation prompted him to connect the U.S. war in Vietnam to the deteriorating conditions in U.S. cities, and of even more consequence, it prompted him to search for more effective tactics in confronting the legal menace of segregation in the North and the attendant crises: slum conditions, unemployment, and police brutality.

Within this context, King began to publicly articulate an anti-capitalist analysis of the United States that put him in sync with rising critiques from the global revolutionary left of market-based economies. Despite the "affluence" of the United States, it was, nevertheless, wracked by poverty and entrenched in an endless war. King masterfully tore down the wall that the political and economic establishments used to separate domestic policies from foreign policies. He debunked the lie at the core of the Johnson administration that they could deliver both guns and butter, and he pointed out how the Vietnam War made it impossible to satisfy the deep need that existed on the home front. Moreover, any society invested in the evisceration of the Vietnamese people could not truly be a society committed to developing the human potential of its own people.

King's realization was the need for even greater forces to be recruited into the movement to achieve social transformation within the United States. By the end of his life, as Terry suggests, King recognized the coercive power of other forms of disobedience. In planning a Poor

People's March in Washington, D.C., he called for *extralegal* protests not aimed at undoing unjust laws, but in the name of political and economic demands that represented the interests of the majority. In Memphis, during the sanitation workers strike in 1968, he called for a *general* strike to shut down the entire city.

In a story published a week before his assassination, King told Jose Yglesias in the *New York Times* magazine, "In a sense you could say we are engaged in the class struggle." The civil rights movement had not cost a dime, he said, but the movement to uproot poverty and inequality throughout the country would "be a long and difficult struggle, for our program calls for a redistribution of economic power." Even as King recognized the need for a broader, multiracial struggle to successfully engage in a "radical revolution of values," he still understood the dialectic connecting the black movement to a larger reckoning in the United States.

He was cut down before he could see the fulfillment of his new strategy in Memphis or in Washington, D.C., and the "interrelated flaws" of U.S. society have only intensified in the fifty years since King first invoked them. Indeed, the conditions warranting class struggle have become worse as the wealth within U.S. society has continued to accrue at the top. Yet King's ability to name the elemental human suffering that is produced by our profit system, while simultaneously demonstrating the centrality of the black movement in unraveling its internal and external logic, remains a powerful political tool. This anniversary, as Terry argues, offers new opportunities to engage King's political thought, including his anti-capitalism and his repeated call for larger and deeper political struggle.

Diagnosing Racial Capitalism

Andrew Douglas

"I AM CONVINCED," Martin Luther King, Jr., said in 1967, "that if we are to get on the right side of the world revolution, we as a nation must undergo a radical revolution of values." This is one of the more resounding lines from King's corpus and one of the most frequently cited. It is often taken to capture the essence of King's later radicalism, a sense of the political commitment and moral urgency that he ascribed to a second, more "substantive" phase of his life's work: to organize an assault on the "evil triplets," the racism, violence, and cycles of impoverishment that, like a kind of organic compound, had conspired to give life force to the only U.S. society the world had yet known.

It is no secret that King became increasingly outspoken in his dissatisfaction with capitalism, especially the ways in which racism and violence had been interwoven into the structural workings of the U.S. economy. But if, as Brandon Terry suggests, King can still help us to "radically challenge" the United States' congenital deformities, and if, as King himself has suggested, any political prescription "rests with the accurate diagnosis of the disease," then we might reflect a bit more on the nature, and legacy, of King's mature critique of capitalism. How is King's call for a "revolution of values" affected by the production and circulation of value in capitalist society?

Though King's analysis moved beyond, and often against, key assumptions and conceptual tools of Marxist thought, Karl Marx's way of thinking about capital as "value in motion" is suggestive and broadly consistent with King's thinking. Consider Marx's account of how the "commodity-form" under capitalism, what we might describe as the market actor's singular and largely compulsory focus on the exchange of money, "conceals a social relation." Marx argued that the coordination of human labor and activity, indeed the kinds of human interdependencies that King cataloged under the rubric of an "inescapable network of mutuality," had become sustained in the modern world by a logic of capital accumulation, by a distinctive pressure put upon market actors to base decisions largely on information available through price signals, and to pursue not only profit, but also sustained growth through the creation of viable outlets for reinvestment. What we are compelled to value and devalue in capitalist society is largely dependent upon its commodification and movement through cycles of accumulation and reinvestment. This movement, this "value in motion," is itself dependent upon the reproduction of social inequalities, which have significant temporal and spatial dimensions, as well as discernible racial dimensions.

As Jodi Melamed reminds us, "Capital can only be capital when it is accumulating, and it can only accumulate by producing and moving through relations of severe inequality among human groups." Such accumulation requires "loss, disposability, and the unequal differentiation of human value, and racism enshrines the inequalities that capitalism requires." Melamed also points out, following Ruth Wilson Gilmore, that the racial inequalities historically endemic to the circulation of capital are reproduced through "technologies of anti-relationality," or normalized, and normally disavowed, processes by which "forms of humanity are separated (made 'distinct') so that they may be 'interconnected' in terms that feed capital." Part of the point here is that any prospect for collective life, any chance for authentic and racially integrated human and democratic interaction, is routinely delimited by territorialization, ghettoization, incarceration, various modes of racialized partition that condition the possibility of "world-systems of profit and governance." The type of critical analysis that can help to expose this—what we might refer to, following Cedric Robinson, as the critical theory of racial capitalism—is broadly consistent with, if not implied by, King's later attentiveness to the economic geographies of racial segregation or the ways in which, as King put it in 1967, "depressed living standards for Negroes . . . are a structural part of the economic system in the United States."

Terry is right to say that, for King, any adequate challenge to racism requires consideration of psychological and ideological as well as sociopolitical factors. But we need to reconstruct King's dissatisfaction with capitalism in order to build out this latter dimension, which is so often missed by conventional projections of King as a kind of idealist or moral philosopher. That our human relationships are mediated by commercial society and its value-form—that, as King so often lamented, we have become a "thing-oriented" rather than a "person-oriented society"—is no mere illusion. If what appears before us is a world marked by "material relations between persons and social relations between things," such relations appear, as Marx famously put it, "*as what they really are*." Under capitalism, our failure to see, to respect, and to make decisions based upon genuinely human interactions, indeed our failure to treat other people as human beings, is less a psychological or epistemic failure than a structured impossibility.

And so perhaps the task in front of us, the prescription that a "second phase" diagnosis calls for, is not merely to recover our morality or to will ourselves to treat human beings as human beings rather than as things. In order even to put ourselves in a position to cultivate this sort of collective memory and will, we need a wholesale transformation of the sociopolitical form of domination, what King referred to as a "restructuring of the whole of American society." Perhaps what we need, more proximately, is a mode of apprehension that can include but also push beyond the epistemic, beyond efforts to debunk racist ideology and false consciousness, as important as such efforts are, and out into the ontological, into a political confrontation with what Robinson has called the "actual being" of racial capitalism.

So, to extend the spirit of Terry's analysis, I suggest that we consider, as an integral part of the King legacy, the question of how King's call for a revolution of values is complicated by the production and circulation of value in capitalist society. In his outward pronouncements at least, King often projected an assurance that "there is nothing except a tragic death wish to prevent us from reordering our priorities." But surely the obstacles, from ideological and fetishistic obfuscation to the emboldened interests of counterrevolution, are far more formidable, far more complex, than King let on.

This, of course, King knew all-too well. In the last years of his life especially, King battled privately through fits of depression and a recurring sense that he was chasing a fool's errand. Many in his inner circle, including veteran anti-capitalist soldiers such as Bayard Rustin and Stanley Levison, sought to persuade King that the United States was just not yet ready for radical political-economic restructuring. And yet King soldiered on. Part of what he gave us, in the last years especially, was the rudiments of a compelling and generative critical theory, a diagnostic account of racial capitalism. This was no fool's errand. Perhaps now more than ever, King's critique can help to motivate incisive thinking about the obstacles that foreclose realization of a more just world as well as the enduring activist legacy of the black radical tradition.

A National Problem

Jeanne Theoharis

THE "COSTS OF CANONIZATION" of Martin Luther King, Jr., as Brandon Terry notes, have been the stripping of much of the civil rights leader's political thought and praxis. We cherry-pick the quotes, refusing the broader indictment he leveled at the country. And we trap King in the South, missing his challenge to northern injustice and the limits of American liberalism from the beginning of the 1960s.

Our popular rendering of King makes it seem like he only recognized the racial problem outside of the South after the 1965 Watts riots. Yet King had crisscrossed the North and West in the early 1960s, joining with movements there and criticizing the willful disregard of black protest long before the uprisings. He was severely attacked for it—often, as he pointed out, by people who supported his work in the South. King doubled down, insisting that racial problems outside the South did not begin with the riots of the mid-1960s—as citizens, political officials, and the media suggested—but with the long history of injustice and frustrated black struggle that preceded them. Ignoring this component of King's activism furthers the myth, popular then and now, that U.S. racism is peculiarly southern, brutal, and redneck rather than national, firm, and stubborn.

In a 1960 speech in New York, King made clear that racism "is not a sectional but a national problem" and called for "a liberalism in the North that is truly liberal, that firmly believes in integration in its own community as well as in the deep South." Over the next few years, King crisscrossed the country, taking part in rallies, meetings, and marches that highlighted the scourge of school and housing segregation, job discrimination, and police brutality outside the South. While his efforts in the South were praised by many in these cities, whites balked as soon as he called out *local* inequality.

Take Los Angeles. In 1961 King made the first of many trips to the city to join with a growing freedom movement in the city around job discrimination, housing and school segregation, and police brutality, speaking before a crowd of 28,000. He returned again in May 1963, addressing 35,000 people at Wrigley Field: "You asked me what Los Angeles can do to help us in Birmingham. The most important thing that you can do is to set Los Angeles free because you have segregation and discrimination here, and police brutality." In 1964 Los Angeles's freedom movement had to shift its energies to defeat a menacing ballot initiative. Proposition 14 sought to repeal California's new Rumford Housing Act, which banned racial discrimination in the sale and rental of property—a law activists had fought for years to achieve. King came multiple times to join the fight, saying its passage would be "one of the most shameful developments in our nation's history." Many white Angelenos labeled him a communist for this work against their "property rights," picketing with signs such as "King Has Hate, Does Travel."

In November 1964, 75 percent of white Californians "voted for ghettos," as King put it: Proposition 14 passed by a two-to-one margin, even as Californians voted by a similar margin to return Lyndon

Johnson to the White House. The message was stark: civil rights were good, as long as they did not come home to California.

This was true in New York and Boston as well. After people rose up in Harlem in 1964 when a police officer killed fifteen-year-old James Powell, King called for a civilian review board that would make police accountable to the public. City leaders basically ran him out of town. Similarly King made multiple trips to Boston in the mid-1960s to join a burgeoning school desegregation movement there. He met with Boston's school committee to urge desegregation, but organizer Ellen Jackson described the meeting, which lasted less than an hour, as a "disaster."

A long history of struggle and civil rights organizing preceded the uprisings of the mid-1960s in cities across the North and West but this is not the way the decade is remembered. King himself repeatedly reframed the issue of riots before northern audiences, highlighting the long history of ignoring black grievances and countenancing systemic injustice.

> [A] riot is the language of the unheard. And what is it America has failed to hear? It has failed to hear that the plight of the Negro poor has worsened over the last twelve or fifteen years. It has failed to hear that the promises of freedom and justice have not been met. And it has failed to hear that large segments of white society are more concerned about tranquility and the status quo than about justice and humanity.

King flipped the question of whether blacks were breaking the law by zeroing in on the white illegality that produced unjust conditions in the first place:

> When we ask Negroes to abide by the law, let us also demand that the white man abide by law in the ghettos. Day-in and day-out he violates welfare laws to deprive the poor of their meager allotments; he flagrantly violates building codes and regulations; his police make a mockery of law.

King thus made clear that a focus on black criminality was both a way to take attention away from white culpability and a way to blame black people for their own situation. Rejecting the cultural arguments that officials and white citizens proffered to explain black poverty, he instead faulted the "white majority . . . [for] producing chaos" and repudiated the notion that if black people simply behaved better, success would come. He took U.S. social science to task for its focus on cultural explanations for inequality: "All too many white Americans are horrified not with conditions of Negro life but with the product of these conditions—the Negro himself."

Fundamentally King understood black rebellion as a rational response to the bad faith of white liberals.

> Negroes have proceeded from a premise that equality means what it says, and they have taken white Americans at their word when they talked of it as an objective. But most whites in America in 1967, including many persons of goodwill, proceed from a premise that equality is a loose expression for improvement. White America is not even psychologically organized to close the gap—essentially, it seeks only to make it less painful and less obvious but in most respects retain it.

But these aspects of King's philosophy—his critique of the North for its disingenuous embrace of black southern activism and its tolerance of white illegality—are too often jettisoned in our national celebrations of him. We prefer to celebrate a King who focuses on southern racists than one who exposes the limits of northern anti-racism, one who dreams about black and white together rather than exposes the cruel illogic of liberal explanations for inequality.

On Violence and Nonviolence

Elizabeth Hinton

IN THE MONTH following the assassination of Martin Luther King, Jr., black uprisings erupted in more than 125 cities, leading to 50 deaths and more than 15,000 arrests. In the years that followed (1968–72), at least 960 segregated black communities witnessed 2,310 separate incidents of what journalists and state security officials described as "disturbances," "uprisings," "rebellions," "melees," "eruptions," or "riots." This type of collective violence almost always started with contact between residents and the frontline representatives of the state—the police—and then quickly moved to other institutions. Indeed, following King's murder, many black residents in cities across the United States responded to the process of criminalization and unanswered calls for greater socioeconomic inclusion by throwing rocks and punches at police officers, detonating firebombs, and plundering local stores.

Although this period of unrest remains marked in many people's memories of the period, it was hardly the beginning of violent urban uprising by black Americans. In fact, U.S. cities had been beset with black rebellion since the enactment of the Civil Rights Act of 1964.

Federal policymakers and officials blamed this earlier period of disorders (and the hundreds of millions of dollars in property damage it caused) primarily on the behavior of young black men. They sought to address it as a criminal problem, launching the War on Crime and passing the Omnibus Crime Control and Safe Streets Act of 1968, which incentivized increased local policing and surveillance of black urban areas, as well as formal "riot control" training. However, a proper understanding of sixties-era urban rebellion depends on our ability to interpret it not as a wave of criminality, but as a period of sustained political violence.

Arguably, the success of King's brand of nonviolent direct political action depended on the presence of this *violent* direct political action. As King recognized, and Brandon Terry points out, the coercive power of mass nonviolence arose in part from its ability to suggest the possibility of violent resistance should demands not be met. Therefore, we should endeavor to see violent and nonviolent expressions of black protest as entwined forces that shaped the decade. In addition, and more challenging perhaps, we should attempt to understand violent rebellion on its own terms, as a form of direct political action that was just as integral to the decade.

It can be a struggle to imagine some of the most overpoliced, marginalized, and isolated Americans as political actors, and this bias has influenced the writing of history. Even those of us interested in forms of resistance to structural racism have been reluctant to take seriously the political nature of midcentury black uprisings. Yet they were neither spontaneous nor "meaningless" eruptions. Just as much as nonviolent direct action, rebellion presented a way for the oppressed and disenfranchised to express collective solidarity in the face of punitive state forces, exploitative institutions, and calcified "democratic" institutions.

Reviving our knowledge of midcentury violent rebellion against police and state forces also has important ramifications on how we tell the history of the rise of mass incarceration. Some scholars of the rise of the carceral state, including Michael Javen Fortner and James Forman, Jr., have recently argued that black Americans called for more police on the streets, at schools, and in housing projects. These accounts, implicitly or explicitly, suggest that black Americans championed the politics of law and order and are therefore partly to blame for the punitive turn in domestic policy. But the history of the forgotten rebellions adds another, dynamic layer and set of actors to the story of the so-called "black silent majority." As much as some segments of the black middle class, political leaders, and clergy joined the clamor for "law and order," many others—who do not appear in traditional archives and many of whom were too young to vote—collectively defied the legitimacy of new policing and carceral strategies.

In addition to the failure to attend to the voices of African Americans across class strata and outside of traditional archives, a crucial part of the story of how these rebellions became obscured in our memory is bureaucratic. By the late sixties, President Lyndon Johnson's Safe Streets Act and the subsequent militarization of local police effectively quashed any nascent movement of political rebellions by making them matters of *local administration* and *pacification* instead of national political crises. The legislation established an unprecedented 330 million dollar federal investment in crime control that effectively began the process of militarizing local police forces operating in communities that seemed vulnerable to rebellion with surplus weapons from Vietnam, and training them in systematic riot control methods. The act essentially created the infrastructure and punitive apparatus to make smaller police departments—particularly those in deindustrializing cities with a critical mass of black residents—capable of handling uprisings on their own before they became spectacular enough to generate national media or activist attention.

Unfortunately, this legacy remains with us. Rather than responding to violent political rebellion with policy—such as addressing mass unemployment, failing public schools, and inhumane housing conditions—policymakers and officials, from Richard Nixon's War on Crime to the bipartisan War on Drugs to Donald Trump's "Law and Order," have consistently sought to manage the material consequences of socioeconomic problems (e.g., urban decay, drug abuse, and gang violence) with more police, more surveillance, and, eventually, more incarceration. We as a nation still fail to reckon with the wisdom King prophetically offered toward the end of his life: that only "social justice and progress are the absolute guarantors of riot prevention. There is no other answer. Constructive social change will bring certain tranquility; evasions will merely encourage turmoil." Whether expressed externally against racist institutions or internally as gang warfare, until the structural roots of collective violence are addressed as King indicated, spiraling tensions and distrust between police officers and the racially marginalized citizens they are charged with protecting will remain.

Sparking King's Revolution

Bernard E. Harcourt

FIFTY YEARS AGO, Martin Luther King, Jr., protested our country's counterinsurgency war in Vietnam. King passionately decried the bombings and civilian deaths, the destruction of families and villages, and the herding of the population into "concentration camps." King denounced our imperialist arrogance and urged "a radical revolution of values." From the pulpit at Riverside Church in New York City, King declared: "These are revolutionary times." Indeed they were. And if anything, they have become even more so today.

Today the United States continues to govern through counterinsurgency warfare. It is no longer aimed at communists, but this time at Muslims and other persons of color. It is not only in the theater of war, but this time also outside conventional war zones. And it is not only abroad, but this time at home as well. With drone strikes and indefinite detention, total information awareness, and hyper-militarized policing on our streets, the United States today governs others and its own citizens through a generalized counterinsurgency warfare paradigm.

Harcourt

Which is why we would do well, as Brandon Terry urges, to reread King's work with a generous but critical eye—and not just King, but Malcolm X, Assata Shakur, and Audre Lorde, as well as Frantz Fanon, Simone de Beauvoir, Mohandas Gandhi, Michel Foucault, and other critical thinkers. Rather than canonize any one of them—or, for that matter, spend our time defrocking them—we should, as Terry counsels, study their texts and practices of resistance in order to challenge the injustices that surround us today.

King recognized the dual fronts of injustice—abroad and at home—and actively protested both: the inhuman disregard for the Vietnamese women, men, and children sacrificed to U.S. interests and also the intolerable inequalities at home, such that, disproportionately, the men who sacrificed themselves abroad did so in the name of liberties "which they had not found in southwest Georgia and East Harlem."

Terry similarly recognizes the dual fronts today: the indiscriminate "unilateral assassination orders" issued by past and present presidents, the militarized policing against Black Lives Matter protesters, and the massive incarceration of people of color. Terry wants to draw on those who, like King, rose up against injustice and oppression to rethink our present more critically. And in so doing, he productively identifies three areas of King's mature thought.

First, on the question of race, Terry builds on King by identifying "*new* features of our racial order." He negotiates a careful path between the liberal search for intentional discrimination and the pessimistic resignation in front of structural racism. Indeed, I would argue, it is crucial to explore how racial, ethnic, and religious differences are being *reconstructed* today to reshape our political imagination—specifically, to create a new category of "internal enemies" that must be understood through the lens of counterinsurgency warfare strategy. It began early, in the 1960s, with the FBI's COINTELPRO operations and the violent repression of the Black Panthers, but it has now become generalized and pervasive in an unprecedented way.

The newest elements include the FBI's recent designation of "Black Identity Extremist (BIE)" as a target of concern and surveillance. These efforts are transforming the way racial and ethnic differences are being constructed: today, the framework of the internal enemy is displacing that of master/slave, of second-class citizenship, of the ghetto, and of the prison. This has potentially drastic consequences since the counter-insurgency strategy is to *eliminate* internal enemies—not just to enslave or oppress.

Second, on the question of direct action and civil disobedience, King's writings and practices are productive, as Terry suggests, especially in conversation with Gandhi's more holistic notion of *satyagraha*, or insistence on the truth. Though it is crucial in this context not to reify situated practices, even King's. Situated practices of revolt are precisely that, *situated*. Occupy Wall Street, for instance, may have achieved some success, however limited, under the Obama administration, but would face very different challenges under Trump's presidency. Fanon's call for violent insurrection may have been appropriate against a militarized colonial superpower, but would likely backfire in a liberal democracy—even a pseudo-liberal democracy overrun by corporate interests.

We are at all times *en situation*, as Jean-Paul Sartre emphasized. Modalities of revolt that are appropriate in certain contexts may not be in others. Along these lines, even the liberal legal strategies that Terry rightly regards with suspicion may at times be effective. In the first year of the Trump administration, civil rights litigation has been the only effective tool to slow down the Muslim ban, the transgender military ban, and the effort to withhold federal monies from sanctuary cities. Direct action did not match the impact of the attorneys general in Washington and Hawaii suing Trump in federal court. And as Alabama relentlessly seeks to execute a sixty-one-year-old terminally ill man who has languished on death row for thirty years, I still have more faith in a judicial stay than in mass mobilization or a gubernatorial reprieve. As Robin D. G. Kelley argues, there is virtue to a multiplicity of strategies and tactics. "Sometimes we confront power directly," Kelley notes, "other times, we struggle to build power where we are—through collectives, mutual aid, community economic development, and the like."

Third, Terry poses the question of ethical virtues in activism and social life. This inescapably raises deeply subjective matters. I personally tack toward the ethical—believing sincerely in the humanity of others and the fragility of life. I aspire to a justice that is forgiving and that does not define each and every one of us by our weakest acts. I seek to instantiate today the just society that I imagine for tomorrow.

Despite that, I resolutely respect others who rise up even when they deploy tactics I might not. King once declared, "Every [person] of humane convictions must decide on the protest that best suits [their] convictions, *but we must all protest.*" Indeed we must, and in ways that allow each of us to remain true to ourselves. In this respect, I am inspired by Foucault who, after being accused of failing to condemn the Islamic uprising he witnessed in Iran in 1978, laid bare his own personal ethic: to be utterly respectful of those who have the courage to rise up against oppression, and to reserve his intransigence and condemnation for the power that reasserts itself against them.

In the end, I share Terry's call to reread King, alongside other revolutionaries, with respect and a critical eye. That is precisely what we are doing in the public seminar "Uprising 13/13" at Columbia University, which brings together theorists, writers, practitioners, and the public in an effort to nourish our practices of resistance and our courage of conviction. Terry's ambition is admirable: to inspire new ideas and modalities of revolt to help us, in his words, "shape a new world out of our [human] dissatisfaction with injustice." Or, in King's words, to bring about that "radical revolution of values." I would only add: to get us beyond our new paradigm of governing through counterinsurgency warfare, abroad and at home.

Harcourt

A Revolution in Values

Brandon M. Terry

I AM HONORED to engage these thoughtful responses from such a distinguished group and even more honored to be part of a forum that aspires to bring Martin Luther King, Jr.'s thought to bear on our present crises. I focus here on three themes that emerge from the responses: race and political economy; violence and the security state; and political imagination, ethics, and judgment.

ALL RESPONDENTS acknowledge the significance of King's critique of U.S. capitalism and economic inequality, especially the extreme disadvantage of the country's ghetto neighborhoods. Jeanne Theoharis rightly argues that our memory of King obscures the connections he saw between the ideological and material foundations of the Jim Crow South and the practices that built urban ghettos: residential and school segregation, job and housing discrimination, unjust policing and sentencing, social isolation, systemic disinvestment, and political subordination. Andrew Douglas adds that King's critique of a "thing-oriented" society exposes how "racial capitalism" persistently frustrates and forecloses efforts at human connection. Broaching the problem of political economy, Douglas presses "the question of how King's call for a revolution of values is complicated by the production and circulation of value in capitalist society," especially one shot through with racist ideology.

This approach to King helps us imagine, as E. P. Thompson did for England, an expanded domain for political economy—beyond the traditional concerns of trade regulations, monetary policy, labor, and the market—that includes disruptive political action and ethical demands of ordinary citizens. For King, collective action (especially when informed by religious and moral traditions) has the capacity to disrupt and transfigure prevailing circuits of value. This is in part why King insisted that nonviolent mobilization and democratic uprising be arrayed directly against businesses.

Recognizing the importance of such actions for King, Keeanga-Yamahtta Taylor highlights King's advocacy of a general strike during the 1968 Memphis sanitation workers' campaign, as well as his vision for mass direct action during the ill-fated Poor People's Campaign that same year. Missing from Taylor's list is Operation Breadbasket, the Southern Christian Leadership Conference's effort to protest, boycott, and negotiate with leading businesses in major cities with the goal of increasing black employment, black vendor contracts, and corporate contributions to civic programs.

After King's assassination, Operation Breadbasket became most closely identified with Jesse Jackson's personality-centered movement in Chicago and its obsessive focus on racial representation and black capitalism, neither of which flows inevitably from King's aspirational model. Operation Breadbasket's enduring force lies in the fact that concerted political action enabled African American activists and their allies to reroute entrenched pathways of profit, contest arbitrary corporate power, and redirect millions of dollars in jobs and contracts to disadvantaged blacks. Another significant effort to emerge from King's Chicago work was the formation of tenants' unions, which organized to secure (through threat of rent strike and direct action) bargaining recognition, building improvements, and anti-eviction rights directly from large property owners. From these activist energies, King hoped a movement would emerge to restructure the unacknowledged bases of economic value in our society, from municipal boundaries to public schooling, while establishing guaranteed basic income and various schemes for bargaining and arbitration as bulwarks against conventional market outcomes. King did not live long enough to further test and champion these ideas, nor did he develop a more comprehensive theory of how economic injustice is structured by gender injustice. His radical proposals, however, designed to uproot basic presuppositions of U.S. federalism and constitutional law, should spark our contemporary political imagination and surely deserve far greater consideration than they currently receive, even in today's revival of interest in the black radical tradition.

A GREAT DEAL of the urgency behind King's turn to ghetto poverty stems from his horror at the rage, disaffection, alienation, and nihilism of the youth he met during the "long, hot summers" of rebellion between 1965 and 1968. My colleague Elizabeth Hinton not only revisits this period and this population, but also recovers the forgotten history of many minor revolts and the cruel dynamic of unjust state repression and street rebellion cemented in the wake of King's murder. Crucially,

Hinton shares King's investment in excavating the ethical and political dimensions of ghetto youth revolt, and in doing so echoes King's judgment that such "violent revolts are generated by revolting conditions and there is nothing more dangerous than to build a society with a large segment of people who feel they have no stake in it, who feel they have nothing to lose."

While acknowledging the "understandable" fear and sense of menace that riots create (even among blacks who live in ghetto neighborhoods), King nevertheless counseled Americans to "resist the impulse to seize upon the rioter as the exclusive villain." King understood that ghetto looting and revolt contains, despite its ills, a kernel of egalitarianism; the "experience of taking" involves fleetingly "redressing the power imbalance that property [distribution] represents," and its violence is usually an attack against available "symbols of exploitation" or the police. Indeed, King urged police to "cease being occupation troops in the ghetto and start protection residents."

Despite acknowledging their legitimate anger and declaring his solidarity with these youth, King criticized chaotic and episodic revolt. He worried about its self-undermining "sense of futility" in the face of economic injustice, and its inevitable defeat in the face of military and police power. For King, the critical task was to *organize* dissent into ethically sensitive forms of mass protest that stood a fighting chance. "To dislocate the functioning of a city without destroying it can be more effective than a riot," King argued, "because it can be longer lasting, costly to the larger society, but not wantonly destructive."

King worried—and accurately prophesied—that ghetto rioting would "strengthen the right wing of the country" and contribute to a "fascist development" within U.S. politics. Indeed, as Bernard E. Harcourt writes in his response, just as ghetto rebellion in the 1960s intensified the illegal state surveillance, repression, and assassination of activists, most notably through the Federal Bureau of Investigation's COINTELPRO program, our own era's uprisings and violence have apparently given the FBI the license to create the absurdly amorphous category of "Black Identity Extremists." Liberals who, in desperation, have placed their faith in the FBI to save democracy from Donald Trump should bear in mind that the FBI has historically advanced our nation's most pernicious racist repression and is now at the heart of an unprecedented expansion of national security power.

HARCOURT ALSO ADDRESSES the ethical questions raised by political violence. He declares his "respect" for "others who rise up even when they deploy tactics [he] might not" and foregrounds the "deeply subjective" dimensions of ethical commitment. I admire Harcourt's stance, especially its humility, but I harbor two worries. First, as King (and Gandhi, for that matter) argued, how we respond to injustice resounds through "an inescapable network of mutuality, tied into a single garment of destiny." One great difficulty in explicating the ethics of oppressed groups stems from the need to balance our deeply felt personal interests, such as dignity and self-respect, with the claims for consideration, fairness, care, and even mercy that others in and outside the group have on us. King hoped that nonviolent, mass direct action could incorporate these myriad considerations without a "slide to subjectivism," as Charles Taylor might put it. The angst that he suffered throughout his career stemmed from his visceral understanding of how human interconnection was especially heightened among the oppressed: how reckless rebellion could invite indiscriminate group repression, how selfish accommodation could entrench group stigmas of inferiority, and how political violence can tragically delimit the indeterminate horizons of how and with whom the world should be shared.

Fueled by these worries, and devoted to genuine solidarity building, King demonstrated respect for other political philosophies and tactics. Yet this respect was exercised through criticism and engaged disagreement. Thus my second concern. I agree with Harcourt that condemnation and intransigence should rarely be deployed against those resisting oppression, but we cannot lose sight of the importance of critical exchange in a spirit of reciprocity as *itself* a sign of respect for people's abilities to give and respond to reasons. King's engagement with Black Power often reflected this approach to disagreement and remains a model for political debate in an era far too prone to social media bromides, ad hominem argument, and flights of speculation about the motives of our interlocutors.

Finally, I want to respond to ethical questions raised by the discourse of the "politics of respectability." Barbara Ransby, historian of the civil rights movement and mentor for activists today, rightly argues that their rejection of "respectability" stems from the callous use of class, comportment, or sexuality to exclude some from civic equality and even sympathy. Indeed, as political scientist Cathy Cohen has long argued, these axes have constituted internal "boundaries of blackness," a shameful legacy of marginalization in African American political solidarity. Accordingly, I consider King at his least coherent and most counterproductive where he traffics in heterosexism or patriarchal gender norms; among his most admirable moments are those when he breaks with conventional norms of respectability to celebrate the dignity of stigmatized work, the countercultural revolt against consumerism, or the political agency of those that society would write off as criminals, dependents, and deviants.

Nevertheless, contemporary uses of "respectability" as a term of opprobrium are overinclusive. Ransby's invocation of righteous anger is instructive. In reducing arguments against the sustained expression of anger to conformity with "middle-class norms," it implicitly associates righteous anger with the poor and does not take seriously enough the complicated normative debates raised by political emotions, which have been at the heart of theological and ethical disagreements in black letters and black communities (including poor ones), and which are presently the topic of intense debate among philosophers such as Martha Nussbaum and Myisha Cherry. The question is how to evaluate ethical claims and understand their justifications. King's arguments for channeling anger into other emotions are rooted primarily in the idea that anger is corrosive of our *own* abilities to live a good life and not an appeal to assimilation. King's claims that anger undermines the ability to sustain constructive political solidarity, tempts human beings toward unjustified retribution, and blinds us to the ethical demands of others are critical arguments to evaluate on their own terms. They are vital concerns for politics, and for life.

My own judgment on these difficult normative questions is far from settled, but I hope these offerings—and all the essays in this issue—will generate the kind of extended discussion that such ideas deserve in our own desperate struggle to discern where we go from here.

Essays

Baldwin's Lonely Country

Ed Pavlić

ON THE AFTERNOON of April 4, 1968, James Baldwin was relaxing by the pool with actor Billy Dee Williams in a rented house in Palm Springs. Columbia Pictures had put Baldwin up there after commissioning him to write a film adaptation of Alex Haley's *The Autobiography of Malcolm X* (1965); Williams was Baldwin's pick to play Malcolm. The men were listening to Aretha Franklin when the phone rang. Upon hearing the news that Martin Luther King, Jr., had been assassinated, Baldwin collapsed in Williams's arms.

Baldwin had known King since 1957, when the two had met in Atlanta. They had seen each other twice in the previous weeks. Both spoke at Carnegie Hall on February 23 in honor of W. E. B. Du Bois. For the event, Baldwin read aloud from his defense of the Black Power activist Stokely Carmichael, an essay that had recently also been published in the *Manchester Guardian*. And on March 16, along with Marlon Brando, Baldwin introduced King at a fundraiser at Anaheim's Disneyland Hotel.

In Baldwin's estimation, King was struggling to guide what remained of the Freedom Movement, contending with the growing appeal of younger militants such as Carmichael while traveling nonstop to support nonviolent action wherever it showed promise. The Freedom Movement had always been chaotic. But by 1968 it was a volatile tumble of organizations, personalities, and philosophies. All were entangled in an increasingly violent culture, one Baldwin had been warning the country about since the early 1960s, most notably in *The Fire Next Time* (1963). As an artist and as an activist himself, Baldwin was astraddle languages of black assertion that were splintering between generations. Introducing King in Anaheim, Baldwin tried to remind listeners that King and younger activists were working toward compatible goals. Radicals hadn't appeared out of nowhere. Baldwin described the journey from 1955 to 1969 as a "terrible descent." Despite present schisms, he stressed common, righteous origins:

> Kids, including people like Stokely Carmichael, were being beaten with chains and thrown into jail . . . and poor Martin spent most of his time in and out of jail . . . trying to redeem . . . the principle of 'love your neighbor,' the principle of 'if it happens to you it's happening to me,' the principle John Donne talked about, you know, when he said that 'any man's death diminishes me.'

On April 12, three days after King's funeral, Baldwin wrote an overdue letter to a long-time friend, Turkish actor Engin Cezzar. Citing grief, exhaustion, and the perilous political weather of the era, Baldwin wrote that, with so many of his cohort murdered, including Medgar Evers, Malcolm X, and now King, he felt overcome by both a despairing silence and an ethical burden to speak. King's murder made Baldwin feel singled out, dangerously exposed, perhaps the last black public intellectual alive capable of bridging the ideological divides separating the leaders of his generation from those who had emerged since the summer of 1966.

Baldwin's literary fame had been built on a complex and elusive sense of racial reconciliation, drawing together disparate but nonetheless proximate corners of the U.S. reading public. Those connections had been tough enough to forge in books and magazines. Reconcilation in history would be much harder than that. But, as he wrote in *The Fire Next Time*, "human history in general, and Negro history in particular," testified "to nothing less than the perpetual achievement of the impossible."

The Fire Next Time had rocketed Baldwin into the role of public intellectual. Almost from the first, Baldwin employed his celebrity in increasingly politicized ways. Having gained the national spotlight, he gave lectures in support of the Congress of Racial Equality (CORE). The same month that his portrait appeared on the cover of *Time*, May 1963, he made the documentary *Take This Hammer*, which brought attention to black poverty and white gentrification in San Francisco. A week later he led an acrimonious meeting with then–U.S. attorney general Robert F. Kennedy about the dire, national implications of racism and violence in Birmingham. Outspoken in ways that kept him off the podium at the August 28 March on Washington for Jobs and Freedom, Baldwin nonetheless led an accompanying march in Paris and appeared with Brando, Sidney Poitier, Harry Belafonte, and Charlton Heston in a roundtable discussion broadcast live on TV in the United States the evening of the march.

While many continued to think of Baldwin as the spokesperson for a vision of ultimate cross-racial communion such as concluded *The Fire Next Time*, Baldwin's speeches and essays grew increasing direct about the impossibilities of saving the United States from itself. By the time of King's murder, Baldwin had shifted his intellectual focus mainly away from black–white reconciliation to instead undertake a no-less-difficult project: facilitating a conversation connecting younger, more radical black leaders with those of his own generation.

IN MAY 1966, Carmichael was elected to replace John Lewis as national chairman of the Student Nonviolent Coordinating Committee (SNCC). Though both men were nearly the same age and both had been involved in the nonviolent crusades of the early sixties, their political trajectories had diverged dramatically. Raised in rural Alabama, Lewis was a true believer in, and practitioner of, nonviolent resistance as modeled by King. Born in Trinidad and raised in Harlem, Carmichael infused King's movement with more radical forms of political action. His leadership pushed SNCC in the direction of its eventual alliance, under the leadership of H. Rap Brown, with the Black Panthers.

Soon after Carmichael's election, civil rights maverick James Meredith was shot during his one-man march across the state of Mississippi. Organizations such as SNCC, CORE, and the Southern Christian Leadership Conference joined together to complete Meredith's march. As the march grew in size, and succeeded in registering thousands of black voters at courthouses along the route, state officials cast off their strategy to tolerate the marchers. The impasse first appeared in Greenwood, Mississippi, when marchers were refused the right to camp on the grounds of Stone Street Negro School. Carmichael intervened and was arrested. He claimed it was the twenty-seventh time since 1961 that he had been jailed.

When Carmichael emerged from jail, he delivered a speech that, in the words of biographer Peniel Joseph, "transformed the aesthetics of the black freedom struggle and forever altered the course of the civil rights movement." Integration and reconciliation were beside the point: what black people needed, according to Carmichael, was "Black Power." Carmichael and his associate Willie Ricks led the primed crowd in a call and response chant: "What do you want?" "Black Power!" By the time King, having made a short trip to Chicago, returned to join the march, photos of Carmichael's arrest had appeared on front pages of national and international newspapers. Within the week, Carmichael had make his first appearances on *Meet the Press*, *Face the Nation*, and other national TV news shows. Carmichael's lean visage would become the face of the new era of Black Power, which, with its turn away from efforts to awaken the moral conscience of white America, represented a serious challenge to King's vision of cross-racial amelioration.

At the time of Carmichael's election, Baldwin was living in Istanbul, working on *Tell Me How Long the Train's Been Gone* (1968). The novel, a mirror of the times and a meditation on Baldwin's own role in them, tells the story of a famed, bisexual black actor's erotic fascination with a character who advocates for racial revolution.

Hearing news of the shakeup in SNCC, Baldwin's brother David wrote to Baldwin abroad. The new watchword, David said, was Black Power. And the reaction to it by established leaders King and Roy Wilkins (of the NAACP), David wrote, was to run the other way.

Baldwin had seen this shift coming. In his reply to David, he said that he felt duty-bound to do a U.S. lecture tour in which he would encourage tactics less self-destructive than those currently being taken. Given the hardening political course of national politics and increasing violence in the United States, Baldwin anticipated that the leaders of his generation would soon be viewed as irrelevant. Baldwin knew he was not an organizer, he was an artist, but he hoped to advise those who would play active political roles. He said that he would urge the younger generation into concrete acts and away from abstract racial theories, from adopting the most "barbaric of the European myths"—from, in effect, "manipulating the color black, merely to become white."

In February 1968 Baldwin and Carmichael arrived in California almost simultaneously, though for very different reasons. Baldwin was there to write a film about Malcolm X, patron saint of the younger activists, for Columbia Pictures. Carmichael, on the other hand, came to California to present an image of a unified Black Power movement. At a ceremony in Oakland, the Black Panther's Minister of Information, Eldridge Cleaver, would name Carmichael the Black Panther's honorary prime minister. Seeking to validate his role as translator of Malcolm's life and keep the lines of communication open between the generations, Baldwin made a point of being seen with Carmichael about the town.

Meanwhile, clearly doing Baldwin no favors, at the top of its front page on February 21 (the third anniversary of Malcolm's murder), *Variety* stressed that "Baldwin has been outspoken against some of the Negro racial extremists, hence his handling of the 'Malcolm X' script poses an obvious question." Luckily, two days later, the *Los Angeles Free Press* republished Baldwin's article on Carmichael, which had already appeared in the *Manchester Guardian*, and which he would read that same night with King at Carnegie Hall. The *Washington Post* and *St. Petersburg Times* reprinted it the following week. Acting as bridge and interpreter, Baldwin reconnected Carmichael to the mainstream of black history. He argued that, indeed, the salient novelty in Carmichael's concept of "Black Power" was its openness, its honesty. Other than that, Carmichael had "simply dug it up again from where it's been lying since the first slaves hit the gangplank."

On February 27, having been in Los Angeles for less than two weeks, Baldwin wrote his brother about the strange scene of black radicals coming to see him at the Beverly Hills Hotel where Columbia Pictures had initially put him up. He told David that they'd come to ascertain if he was for real because he was in Los Angeles to tell the world about Brother Malcolm. Among those who came to Beverly Hills was Hakim Jamal, soon-to-be founder of the Malcolm X Foundation and cofounder of the radical black nationalist organization US. Jamal was there on assignment with the *Free Press* to do an interview with Baldwin that would run alongside his defense of Carmichael.

Jamal's first question was about Baldwin's years in France: "Why on earth would you go to a country that is predominantly white?" Answering at an angle to his interrogator's intentions, Baldwin responded: "I never thought of it quite in that way before. . . . The people I saw in Paris, I saw from a great distance for a very long time." Jamal continued, "Have you escaped from the ghetto in the United States?" Baldwin: "In a sense, as long as people are in the ghetto, I don't want to escape from it. Where would I go?" Despite the ideological distance, the two established a kind of rhythm, with Jamal trying again and again to box Baldwin in, and Baldwin always escaping the trap. Or not.

> *Jamal:* I asked that because we're in the Beverly Hills Hotel, where if there's five Black people in the whole hotel, it's a miracle—the janitors are all white, the chambermaids are even all white. And you're in what would be considered a bourgeois state right now.
> *Baldwin:* I'm a very bourgeois type.

Throughout the conversation, Baldwin fielded accusatory questions on his toes but also made it clear that he wasn't easy to intimidate.

> *Jamal:* Are you a homosexual?
> *Baldwin:* No, I'm bisexual. Whatever that means.
> *Jamal:* Good. No, I know, because that's what they say anyway.
> *Baldwin:* I don't give a shit what people say.

Turning to Malcolm X, Jamal asked, "Did you know him well?"

Baldwin: I don't know if I knew him well; we loved each other. We were very good friends.

Jamal: I know that.

Baldwin: It's difficult, because now he's dead. If you had asked me when he was alive if I knew him well, I would have said yes. When a man is dead, you wonder how well you knew him, no matter how well you loved him. There was so much more in Malcolm than Malcolm knew how to tell. There was so much more in him than he ever lived to express.

Jamal asked if Baldwin thought that Malcolm X hated white people. Baldwin said no, he didn't think so; Malcolm "understood something about this country and our dilemma here that carried him far past that." Then, Baldwin swerved. In letters to his brother, he'd been rehearsing a response to being challenged, as he knew he would be, over choosing Elia Kazan, a "white man," as the director of a film about Malcolm X. He told his brother that he intended to respond by saying, simply, that no one could *prove* that Kazan was white. In response to the idea of Malcolm hating white people, Baldwin veered into his thoughts about Kazan, whose novel *The Arrangement* (1967) he'd reviewed the previous spring in the *New York Review of Books.* Baldwin told Jamal:

> You said in the beginning that our problem is white against black—but I think in fact our problem is much deeper than that. In the first place, I'm not sure any white man in this country is able to prove he's white. That's a myth. And Negro is a legal term. That's another myth really. The problem in this country is that brothers are tearing each other to pieces and have been doing so for generations.

For Baldwin, the whole mythic racial nightmare was based upon "economic arrangements of the Western world [which] are obsolete."

People's identities as Americans are built on fraudulent terms, terms founded upon criminal economic arrangements. Of the latter, Baldwin told Jamal, "Either the West will revise them or the West will perish." This was especially acute for white folks gripped in "European hangovers" who fantasized that they had more in common with villagers in Scotland or Ireland than they did with black folks who had been their neighbors (and closer than that!) for generations. Economics and race were mutually reinforcing false witnesses. White Americans (and now, in radical response, black folks too) seemed determined to pretend that "race" was a naturally occurring phenomena, and Americans' delusional sense of economics indicated that "mink coats grow and automobiles are an act of God." No matter the myths, as for the cars at least, Baldwin reminded: "they're all built out of stolen tin." People around the world in places such as Johannesburg are not going to go down into mines, "dig up all that wealth, and give it away. That is simply not going to go on forever."

But in economics and likewise with the identities of human beings, pretending that such things were matters of nature and would, therefore, "go on forever" required performances worthy of Oscars. Baldwin said that all of this makes "John Wayne the ideal. He's a straight-shooter. A simple, straight-forward guy. You can trust him. Only trouble is, he's brainless." Meanwhile, riffing on Du Bois's idea of double consciousness, Baldwin stressed that an "American male who is capable of having two warring thoughts at the same time is suspect." This delusional mash up of economics, identity, and simple-mindedness was a recipe for exactly the national electoral politics of the era, as well as the radical responses to it.

Jamal was following along, kind of: "Yes, it's true that most Americans live with contradictions." Baldwin pushed the conversation further.

Yes, but they lie about them. It's the loneliest country in the world because everybody is saying to his neighbor what he thinks his neighbor wants him to say. Then they have violent nervous breakdowns all of a sudden, and they murder their children or their wives and everyone wonders why. They've been carrying this thing around in them all along and suddenly it blows up. People are not what we say they are. People are much more complex than that. If you think that's what people are, then you get Washington. Then you get that cretin in the White House. What is his virtue if he's not straight-forward, hard-hitting, simple-minded, patriotic, our American boys and all that bull-shit?

Despite his intensity, Baldwin took pains to make sure that the conversation did not read as a generational battle—quite the opposite. In a way most of the radical leaders in the younger generation did not expect, Baldwin respected them and he feared for their dangerous predicament, one made all the more dangerous by what he regarded as *his* generation's failures.

Four years ago. It seems like a thousand years ago. And all of us four years ago hoped—though we might have had other suspicions—that we could prevent what has come. But we couldn't. We tried. We failed.

In a way he considered very *un*-American, Baldwin understood that generations depend upon each other. When Jamal pointed out a disagreement he perceived between Baldwin and Brown, Baldwin answered: "Well, Rap and I are very different people. I'm much older than Rap." Reading now, we think we can see what's coming: the elder deploys his wisdom. Instead, Baldwin continues, "and Rap may know a lot that I don't know."

What if Baldwin could have indicated to Jamal that militaristic titles and shotguns were not going to atone for the massacre of his generation of leaders? That beards and berets, new names and new holidays were not going to seize the day? That historical horrors were alive behind the lines, at work in intimate proximities and, yes, in contradictions, the existence of which Americans are warned away from admitting? In a way which Baldwin understood, it would have been impossible to make such counsel, and presumptuous for him to try. Of Carmichael Baldwin wrote:

> I get his message. . . . a black man under thirty, is saying to me, a black man over forty, that he will not live the life I've lived, or be corralled into some of the awful choices that I have been forced to make. And he is perfectly right.

A week before King was slain in Memphis amid a strike by sanitation workers, Baldwin told his brother that he just didn't care about the country like he once did. He examined the looming catastrophes and figured most Americans deserved it. The only trouble was that some *didn't*. And that pretty much covers Baldwin's vision circa 1968. He hoped to transfer a depth of concern and restraint, an incisive and tactical maturity, a force (he called it love) forged by his generation and ones preceding, to the next generation of black people and whomever else—not a mass movement—might be out there listening. King and his legions really had tried to inject some substance from that vision into the country as a whole; they'd been met with rejection, duplicity, and lethal violence. So be it, Baldwin thought, and he went ahead.

Throughout the early seventies, Baldwin would continue to support Black Power activists such as Huey Newton, Bobby Seale, Angela Davis, George and Jonathan Jackson, and Amiri Baraka. He'd also support the work of emerging writers such as Toni Morrison, Gayl Jones, and Maya Angelou. He'd even entertain pleas from Eldridge Cleaver, even though he had called Baldwin an untrustworthy faggot in his book *Soul on Ice* (1968). Baldwin's work would never again address itself in good faith to people who still insisted—in light of it all—that they were *white*. In spite of this, Baldwin's writing over the next two decades—until his death in late 1987—would continue to develop its singularly nuanced vision of human capacity and possibility. U.S. political and literary ambition would drift elsewhere until, in recent years, another generation of activists in the Movement for Black Lives, and another generation (or two) of black artists—among them Ta-Nehisi Coates, Claudia Rankine, Jesmyn Ward, Kiese Laymon, and Barry Jenkins—would turn back to examine more closely what Baldwin had wrought, in complex and conflicted hopes up until 1968, and in politicized repudiation of despair thereafter.

BY THE END of 1968, Baldwin had decided that he couldn't work with the agenda of the movie industry. He finished his script nonetheless and would publish it as *One Day, When I Was Lost* (1972). But by then Columbia Pictures had moved on, and so had Baldwin. Of the experience, he would later write in *The Devil Finds Work* (1976), "I would rather be horsewhipped, or incarcerated in the forthright bedlam of Bellevue, than repeat the adventure." Either as a parting gesture or as a last-ditch effort to apply pressure, Baldwin announced the impasse in the *New York Times* on February 2, 1969. In his op-ed, Baldwin explained that he would only feel the film was a success if it depicted Malcolm's "public discontent" and "daily danger" while also showing "the private dimensions of his disaster." But, as Baldwin came to realize, there was a problem: "How, given the conditions of his life here, is he to distinguish between the two?" Baldwin concluded that "there may not be a distinction and that may be the moral of the tale." But the Hollywood agenda, in full view in Sidney Poitier's recent films, was to find "a way of involving, or incorporating, the black face into the national fantasy in such a way that the fantasy will be left unchanged and the social structure untouched." Baldwin thought that everything about the United States needed to be changed. And, from his point of view, just about every citizen was desperate to be—and terrified of being—touched.

The trouble extended well beyond Hollywood. Baldwin's generation had been decimated. As far as he could see, the younger generation—people such as Jamal—was headed into revolutionary chaos. Much of the rest of the country was looking for a way to forget it all. Aided by a sophistication in market research new to U.S. politics, Richard Nixon addressed this urge among a "silent center." As Rick Perlstein notes in *Nixonland*, on May 16 then-candidate Nixon gave a national radio address where he described "millions of people in the middle of the U.S. political spectrum who do not demonstrate, who do not picket or protest loudly." Aligning himself with arch-segregationist South Carolina senator Strom Thurman to usher into existence a new Republican Party whose ranks would include millions of formerly Democrat white southerners, Nixon described a "great many quiet Americans . . . committed to answers to social problems that preserve personal freedom." In his editorial for the *New York Times*, Baldwin noted Nixon's "silent center" in "the bulk of this country's white population." Baldwin described it from his perspective:

> They have been white, if I may so put it, too long; they have been married to the lie of white supremacy too long; the effect on their personalities, their lives, their grasp of reality, has been as devastating as the lava which so memorably immobilized the citizens of Pompeii. They are unable to

conceive that their version of reality, which they want me to accept, is an insult to my history and a parody of theirs. . . . [I]f they think that things are more important than people . . . [l]et them be destroyed by their things.

With King dead, Baldwin saw no leader who could any longer speak to what he considered the real needs of the people in the country. For all his brilliance and charisma, Carmichael was not that man. Moreover, Baldwin said that he had no reason to believe that Carmichael would survive another year. The cold and cowardly throng Baldwin was noting among Americans in 1968 would be exactly the population manipulated by Nixon in the name of the "silent majority." Baldwin couldn't identify a leader capable of describing the reality of the United States in terms that were accurate and that would be honorably engaged by the bulk of the population. In a July *Esquire* article, Baldwin's vision of the political terrain in 1968 sadly reads, with a few slight alterations, like contemporary news fifty years later:

> You're going to need somebody who is willing, first of all, to break the stranglehold of what they call the two-party system. . . . What we need is someone who can coalesce the energies in this country, which are now both black *and* white, into another party which can respond to the needs of the people. The Democratic Party cannot do it. . . . I personally will never vote for a Republican as long as Nixon is in that party. You need someone who believes in this country, again, to begin to change it.

From Baldwin's point of view at the time, the best of those who had tried were all dead.

Against National Security Citizenship

Aziz Rana

NO PART of the vision statement for the Movement for Black Lives received as much immediate mainstream pushback as its stinging repudiation of U.S. foreign policy. Its demands, which included a call for military and security divestment, permanent opposition to the War on Terror, and a declaration of solidarity with Palestinians, generated criticism about specific policies (especially with respect to Israel and Palestine) and about the perceived disconnect between police brutality toward black citizens and U.S. military practices in distant lands. The implication was that by extending their vision beyond the national borders, black freedom activists were combining issues that were not inherently connected and better left to the security experts.

Moreover, critics were uncomfortable with the statement's rejection of one of the most common mechanisms for outsider groups to gain inclusion in U.S. life: national security citizenship. By this I mean the idea that one shows one's worthiness for membership by supporting—and being willing to fight and die for—the security policies of the state. To this day, the idea that oppressed groups earn inclusion through sacrifice on behalf of the state remains a potent one. Simply recall Bill Clinton's effort during his 2016 Democratic National Convention speech to reach out to Muslims, a group that had been targeted and demeaned by Donald Trump's campaign. "If you're a Muslim and you love America and freedom and you hate terror," Clinton offered, "stay here and help us win and make a future together." Behind the rosy rhetoric, the clear implication was that Muslim's rights were conditional on their support of U.S. security commitments and that such support was how Muslims cemented their status as Americans.

By contrast, in linking black freedom to *opposition* to the country's foreign policy orientation, the Movement for Black Lives' statement repudiated the classic assumption that the goals of the security state and the goals of oppressed communities should be thought of as one and the same. Instead, it argued, oppressed communities have to articulate their own independent foreign policy grounded above all in the interests of other marginalized groups. As the document reads, "The Black radical tradition has always been rooted in igniting connection across the global south under the recognition that our liberation is intrinsically tied to the liberation of Black and Brown people around the world." This independent orientation emphasizes solidarities abroad (between poor or colonized peoples) and, as a consequence, directly challenges the security state's prerogatives. Suspicious of any harmonious "we the people," freedom activists instead see a shared community emerging, not with fellow co-nationals, but with the oppressed everywhere.

By emphasizing the tie between the foreign and the domestic as well as the need for a distinct black foreign policy, the authors of the vision statement carried on an essential, although often forgotten, element of Martin Luther King, Jr.'s own political legacy. We do not ordinarily think of King as an exemplar of a black and radical internationalism, but in the last year of his life, King went much further than simply declaring his opposition to the Vietnam War. He also declared his hostility to U.S. militarism in all its forms and asserted that such hostility was integral to his account of black freedom.

King saw the war as emblematic of a general U.S. approach to foreign affairs that treated local, often non-white communities as means to the end of national ambitions and as instruments for the perpetual extension of global power. The logic that justified subverting anti-colonial independence movements in Southeast Asia was the very same logic that maintained structures of racial and class subordination at home. It is why he argued, much to the consternation of President Lyndon Johnson and black elites such as Whitney Young at the National Urban League, that one could not coherently promote black freedom while supporting the war. The two issues, he contended, were inextricably intertwined.

Today, King's anti-imperialism is usually either ignored altogether or, more commonly, defanged of precisely what made it so threatening at the time. To the extent that current commentators mention King on U.S. foreign policy, it is only to discuss the war in Vietnam shorn of any of its broader Cold War context and presented in the most conventional terms. Since the war was unpopular, it is not a surprise that King would oppose it. Indeed, the meaning ascribed to King's opposition is often reduced to the common center-left narrative of Vietnam: it was a discrete folly undertaken by an otherwise moral nation.

What is lost is the revolutionary implication behind King's rejection of the totality of U.S. imperium. Since such imperium was an expression of basic flaws in the structure of U.S. society, King's growing belief was that the United States could only be redeemed if it was fundamentally transformed, both at home and abroad. This is a position rarely associated now with the sanitized and sanctified King of popular culture. But for King, as for his radical descendants in the Movement for Black Lives, black freedom cannot be achieved without breaking from U.S. nationalism and articulating a global vision of racial justice. These views were controversial in the 1960s and, as the blowback faced by Black Lives activists or even Colin Kaepernick attests to, they remain deeply unsettling today.

AT THE HEART of U.S. civic nationalism, as I have written elsewhere, is the idea that the United States has been committed to the principle—emblazoned in the Declaration of Independence—that "all men are created equal" and that the country's history can be viewed as a steady fulfillment of this founding promise. In 1944 Swedish sociologist Gunnar Myrdal offered a foundational articulation of this collective ethos, declaring in *An American Dilemma* that "this nation early laid down as the moral basis for its existence the principles of equality and liberty." Myrdal argued that, although racist and archaic practices may have continued to persist in pockets—or entire regions—of the country, these practices were incompatible with national values. "The main trend" in U.S. history was "the gradual realization" of what he called "the American Creed." Indeed, so pure were the country's founding motives that the United States could be seen, at its core, as nothing less than "humanity in miniature."

In the years after World War II and in the context of global competition with the Soviet Union, this vision of national identity increasingly became central to how U.S. policymakers and elites conceived of the collective project. This account was compelling for a number of reasons, chief among them for how it combined, during the height of the Cold War, racial reform with a defense of U.S. power. Because domestic politics were built on universal values, the defense of those values from outside threats and the projection of them abroad could be seen as a good beyond question. As Myrdal had underscored, Americans stood "warmheartedly against oppression in all the world."

Promoting freedom at home was thus used to justify security prerogatives abroad. President Harry Truman explicitly argued that if U.S. foreign ambitions were to succeed, the country would have to "correct the remaining imperfections in our practice of democracy." Against the global backdrop of anti-colonial resistance, President Lyndon Johnson told a trusted advisor that "segregation" at home was "absolutely crazy" because "80 percent of the world is not white." For both presidents, recasting domestic institutions as essentially just, in need of only small-scale reform, buttressed the legitimacy of the U.S. claim to hegemony and to international police power.

This narrative also allowed racial reform to go hand in hand with preserving U.S. domestic stability. Changes were depicted as achieving a set of ideals present since the founding of the republic and requiring no fundamental breaks with the economic and political status quo. It should be noted that this essentially preservative role was shared not just by white politicians but also by some representatives of the black middle class, who had long viewed the civil rights struggle in terms of elite social mobility and of liberal inclusion into arenas of corporate, professional, and political power.

The question of how black and other oppressed groups should relate to U.S. foreign policy was thus clear. Since the country was basically just, its efforts abroad were similarly worthy. Unlike its totalitarian foes—closed and authoritarian states—the United States was an open and tolerant society that spread universal self-government wherever it went. This meant that, regardless of one's race or sense of marginalization domestically, all Americans as a single "we the people" should identify with the country's global authority and overall objectives.

This vision of the national project promoted a clear bargain between white policymakers and the traditional civil rights movement, one with obvious echoes throughout U.S. history. For white and black defenders of racial equality, war support and participation—national security citizenship—had long been a means to justify black inclusion. From Crispus Attucks, the first person killed during the American Revolution, to the black regiments that fought for the Union Army, to the "Buffalo Soldiers" that participated in military campaigns against native peoples, identifying with the state's imperatives served as proof of one's belonging.

Similarly, in the Cold War years, black activists were being asked to parrot a patriotic anti-communism and to defend U.S. global power as a condition, often explicitly, of implementing domestic reforms. As proof of this bargain, look no further than the State Department's involvement in *Brown v. Board of Education* (1954), in which the department submitted an amicus brief emphasizing the importance of overturning segregation as part of winning hearts and minds in the struggle with the Soviet Union.

When U.S. power seemed to align with anti-racism, the tensions embedded in such national security citizenship dissipated. During World War II, African American leaders routinely tied the war against Nazism to the domestic struggle against white supremacy—viewing these opponents as two sides of the same coin and calling for a "double victory" over fascism. Under these conditions, the call among black leaders to "close ranks," as W. E. B. Du Bois infamously declared during World War I, was less fraught.

But what if the conflict required blacks to support a war effort that promoted racial hegemony and European empire and that undermined the ability of other oppressed and non-white groups to enjoy self-rule? When African Americans fought and died to expropriate land from native peoples or to maintain power over a colonized Filipino population, did that not promote precisely the politics of white supremacy that shackled them at home? More than anything else, this was the dilemma that Vietnam raised for the civil rights movement.

ULTIMATELY, the only way for King to take this basic problem seriously was to move beyond the civic and creedal nationalism that defined the Cold War racial compact. But this is not how he is remembered today. Americans at present tend to think of the King who, in 1961, referred to the Declaration of Independence as the "noble dream" of the Founding Fathers even though the enduring truth of the U.S. project was "as yet unfulfilled." This early King seemed to accept Cold War patriotism, viewing the "American dream" as what "ultimately distinguishes democracy and our form of government from all of the totalitarian regimes that emerge in history."

But King's rhetorical embrace of creedal language was part of a long-standing ambiguity in black political thought. A century earlier, Frederick Douglass had both declared that the Constitution was an anti-slavery document committed to universal principles and had spoken on July 5, 1852, to vigorously assert the constitutive racism of the U.S. project in his speech "The Meaning of July Fourth for the Negro." Douglass both embraced and disavowed a universally egalitarian account of U.S. identity as the "truth" of the national project, and he realized that whenever he invoked U.S. principles he was in part seeking to call into being a national ethos that may not actually exist. Similarly for King, proclaiming the "American dream" to be true was tied to his rhetorical effort to compel white America to reconceive the meaning of its own project.

But what Vietnam eventually highlighted for King was that completing the civic national project alone may not be enough to generate ultimate liberation for black and oppressed peoples. As King noted in his 1967 speech on the conflict, the Vietnamese "must see Americans as strange liberators," given that the United States had "vigorously supported the French in their abortive effort to recolonize Vietnam" and now was brutally imposing its own economic and security ends on an indigenous people seeking independence. As he would repeat over the next year, U.S. behavior in Vietnam was a product of the general structure of U.S. institutions. Rather than essentially just, these institutions had long been organized on principles of class and racial hierarchy. As a result, the security prerogatives that the state projected abroad were necessary extensions of these domestic hierarchies.

In contrast to the creedal nationalism of the traditional civil rights movement, King began articulating his own version of Third World Internationalism, an orientation that had for decades shaped much of radical black politics. Such "third worldism" viewed the United States not as a quintessentially free and equal nation, but instead through the struggles against colonialism that were engulfing the Global South. According to this perspective, the United States was divided between racially privileged insiders and nonwhite peoples, whose land and labor served as the basis for elite wealth and power. As in apartheid South Africa, the fact that U.S. society was founded on oppression meant that liberation would require more than inclusion in the existing social order; it would necessitate precisely what King called for, a "radical restructuring" or a "revolution in values."

The United States' ongoing relationship with South Africa was eye-opening for King, and he emphasized how the United States played a vital role in sustaining white rule there: "the tragedy of South Africa is not simply in its own policy; it is the fact that the racist government of South Africa is virtually made possible by the economic policies of the United States and Great Britain."

Such uncomfortable facts led King to a remarkable conclusion. The standard liberal anti-war position then—as it is today in the context of Iraq or Afghanistan—was to critique the conflict as inconsistent with the nation's moral fabric. But King took his criticism further. In the war, he saw a deep truth about the violence encoded in the country's very DNA. For that reason, not only was the war in Vietnam unjust, but black support for Cold War imperatives as such were morally indefensible. At a time when "all over the globe men are revolting against old systems of exploitation and oppression," Cold War anti-communism placed a false patriotism ahead of meaningful solidarities between poor and excluded peoples.

Thus, "a genuine revolution of values" meant "that our loyalties must become ecumenical rather than sectional" and that black and poor communities had to reject a warlike nationalism in favor of properly internationalist alliances of shared interest and commitment. At home, this required reimagining the civil rights movement as a poor people's movement that incorporated blacks, impoverished whites, indigenous peoples, and immigrant communities with the goal of abolishing poverty and overcoming capitalism. And with respect to Vietnam, it underscored that people of good conscience could not participate in the conflict and should explicitly seek conscientious objector status—even if they may be able to claim other exemptions—to avoid the draft.

King did not go as far as the Black Panthers to contend that black people, as an internally colonized group, should not have to serve in the military at all. But his call to refuse the draft on ideological grounds and to reject the security state altogether was nonetheless dramatic. It was also a profoundly difficult call for him to make, especially given his access to the highest echelons of white politics. It entailed breaking from the bargain that marked national security citizenship and that allowed for inclusion, albeit on terms of black assimilation, into the economic, political, and military status quo. It raised the specter of African Americans, as had long been the case, being cast yet again as a "fifth column" in the United States and as inherently anti-American. Indeed, especially after King's assassination, the U.S. government escalated its crackdown on black radicalism—with leaders killed, imprisoned, or forced into exile—and justified its actions in precisely these terms.

But for King the imperative was clear. The civic nationalism of the Cold War and its constitutional faith was ultimately insufficient to dislodge "the giant triplets of racism, materialism, and militarism." In King's view, the country, particularly in its embrace of the corporate and security implications of the "American century," had chosen "by choice or by accident" a destructive historical path: "the role of those who make peaceful revolution impossible by refusing to give up the privileges and pleasures that come from the immense profits of overseas investments." Ultimately, any actual justice would necessitate transcending the creed and even the "American dream" he had spoken about so eloquently; the nation had to be transformed, root and branch, into a fundamentally new polity.

TODAY THE VERY REASONS why King broke from the strictures of national security citizenship are evident throughout the political landscape. Whatever its rhetorical appeal, such strictures have come at real costs, over time dramatically narrowing the boundaries of political conversation and sustaining a conservative and hierarchical nationalism. We can see these costs in the role U.S. militarism plays in shaping the terms of acceptable patriotism and in silencing dissent generally, from black athletes kneeling for the national anthem (so as to protest ongoing racial oppression) to Muslim and Arab Americans questioning the mass surveillance of their communities as well as the legitimacy of U.S. policy in the Middle East.

We also see the costs of the supposed termination of formalized discrimination—the heart of the postwar racial bargain. Indeed, civil rights protections have not generated a post-racial country, but have instead gone hand in hand with hyperincarceration of communities of color, extreme class inequalities, and the increasing return of an explicit and virulent white supremacy. The failure since King's death to address the structural dimensions of racial and class subordination—as well as the persistent growth of the security apparatus—has left those "giant triplets" he railed against unchecked in U.S. life.

As the left grows more assertive against the backdrop of centrist defeat and in the era of Trump and Republican xenophobia, any truly progressive social base must be built on a vision of solidarity that rejects false nationalisms and that connects arguments about U.S. power to those about political economy. We have seen this emerge already not only in the Movement for Black Lives, but also in the Occupy movement, elements of the 2016 Bernie Sanders campaign, the Moral Monday protests in North Carolina, the Fight for Fifteen, and the efforts at a genuine cooperative commonwealth in Jackson, Mississippi.

King recognized a half century ago that liberal completion would not effectively redeem the country, but we are trapped today with the consequences of that failed path. We still require that same radical re-structuring that King suggested in the months before his death—one that calls out capitalism and empire as the relevant forces of oppression and that sees a cross-racial and class conscious movement as the only foundation for effective freedom.

1968 and the Crisis of Liberalism

Samuel Moyn

FOR A LONG TIME, a faction of U.S. liberals shouldered the burdens of a fully inclusive social compact. They rightly indicted welfare-state compromises that served some and not others, and that served even the most privileged beneficiaries—white working-class men—only to some extent. Recognizing that the New Deal was a raw one for the neglected poor as well as African Americans and women, some liberals in the early and mid-1960s gave sustained critique to the structural limitations of New Deal liberalism and the Cold War geopolitics that framed the enterprise.

After 1968, disaster set in. Faced with the sins of Vietnam, the Democrats flirted with ending Cold War militarism only to double down on it. The critique of the welfare state, not the demand for its extension, prevailed. A toxic brew of white identity politics, a rhetoric of "family values" and "personal responsibility," and, above all, anti-statist economics wafted across party lines. Fifty years later, Donald Trump is in the White House, embattled but victorious.

How did we get here? Much depends on how one narrates the path from 1968 to Trump's election.

Mark Lilla's book of last year, *The Once and Future Liberal*—a follow-up to his hugely influential *New York Times* op-ed "The End of Identity Liberalism," published days after Trump's win—has gone far toward defining the terms of that story. But instead of looking carefully at how liberal self-reinvention failed in facing down its scurrilous enemies, Lilla cuts off his enterprise in a dodge. Lilla thinks that U.S. welfare-state liberalism was doomed in the 1970s, when its neoconservative enemies rightly sounded its death knell. He goes on to report that the heirs of the raucous sixties, failing to reinvent liberalism beyond its prior statist limits, embraced the anti- and pseudo-politics of "identity." For much of the book, indulging his Francophile proclivities, Lilla channels the moralist Alexis de Tocqueville, blaming our contemporary degeneration on a culture of narcissism, adding a whiff of the novelist Michel Houellebecq in unmasking the "real" legacy of the sixties as a journey into the interior. A cult of the self prospered as politics died.

Even though Lilla has told much of this story before, there is actually something new and promising in this book. It is not his ill-conceived and unpersuasive indictment of identity politics, but his case that U.S. liberalism must take a turn to face structural realities if it is to save itself. His own version of what that requires—building a new nationalism—fails badly, but the insight is dead on. Yet in the barrage of attention *The Once and Future Liberal* has received, the premise that points far beyond Lilla's own analysis has not even been noticed.

For an author known for much of his career as a scourge of the left, Lilla's reliance on Karl Marx to drive his argument is curious. Over the course of the short text, he makes not one but two section-length shout-outs to Marx—and they are utterly pivotal. Lilla appeals to "material conditions" to explain what politics are plausible in any particular time period and—above all—how it was that progressives drifted into an unholy alliance with the right they were supposed to be fighting. Too bad Lilla does not follow through on that insight. If he did so, we would have more of the explanation we need, and the story of what happened between 1968 and Trump would be about economics and politics, and not solely about culture.

"If an ideology endures," Lilla explains, "this means it is capturing something important in social reality." And in Lilla's story, it was no accident that the left embraced an individualism—embarking on searches for meaning and obsessed with their personal identities—that atomized the country at the same time that the right championed a parallel economic libertarianism. Identity politics is "Reaganism for lefties," Lilla says, just with self-absorption rather than self-interest as the rationale. Beaten in their initial demands for a collective justice beyond the limits of the old welfare state, refugees from the 1960s took over the English departments and taught their students not communitarian politics but wounded narcissism.

Lilla is right that material conditions strongly affect the imaginations of reformers, even if they do not determine it. Marx made that point most famously, but it is the common coin of all who believe that no one makes history under circumstances of their own choosing. And we are living in times that force a new acceptance of this truth, even if we conclude that the imagination counts alongside interests (indeed, helps define interests) in the making of social reality. Our economically neoliberal age has shaped many of the most exciting causes progressives have embraced in recent decades, helping to tilt them in an individualist and meritocratic direction. These range from an affirmative action that has tended to help the best-off African Americans (along with recent immigrants and their children who fit the terms of the programs); to a feminism that honors the shattering of glass ceilings for elites but not the stagnation of the lives of middle-class and poor women; to an LGBTQ politics that lifted centuries of opprobrium by appealing to the libertarian instincts of constitutional judges.

Indeed, Lilla's feints toward a politics of economic interests distinguish *The Once and Future Liberal* from other once-famous analyses and indictments of atomistic fracture and the "disuniting of America," of identity politics and liberal racism, ranging from Tocqueville himself to Daniel Rodgers or Richard Rorty or Arthur Schlesinger, Jr. But Lilla's overall story of the United States and the Democratic Party is still far too much about the superstructure (in the relevant terminology). It needs more attention to the base. More importantly, it is too much about the wrong reformers, focusing on the New Left in humanities departments and omitting the actual governmental and party policies that have mattered most. Lilla intuits the limits of his culturalist analysis of narcissism, but he discards his newfound acknowledgment that structural forces matter.

START AWAY from campus, to avoid assigning it more than a bit part. Is not the sad drama Democrats have found themselves playing primarily one of their own scripting, most of all on the economic front? Taking neocon lessons about the bloated welfare state, Democrats in platforms and power since the late 1970s have joined Republicans not in the identity politics that Lilla sees as an indirect form of neoliberalism, but in neoliberalism itself. Is the most convincing explanation for the defeat of Hillary Clinton that the Democrats have failed in national politics, or that, in recent history, they have won fully as many times as their supposed rivals, and instituted policies not far from them, thanks to politicians in orbit around the richest monied interests? How strange: Lilla turns to material realities to explain how identity politics are neoliberal, instead of why the *Democratic Party* has been neoliberal, now and for a long time.

If universities matter, it is when they are put within that larger framework, rather than cast as a secret throne room of the party. Lilla's story is that professors went into beaten hibernation in their campus caves after the 1960s. But if that is true, then it does not make sense to say that they simultaneously exerted enormous influence from there. If students have in fact dropped civic engagement to tag each other on Instagram and gave up changing the world for the task of burnishing their resumes (as Lilla says), is it because their teachers misled them or because consumerism accelerated, student debt mounted, and the rat race intensified? For that matter, if the intellectual life of universities needs to be put in receivership for the sake of the country's future, isn't that far more true of economics than of English departments? Who is more at fault for the failure of the Democratic Party to anticipate—let alone manage—the stagnation of the white male working class over the last four decades? Is it Homi Bhabha and Judith Butler—or Lawrence Summers?

It is not even clear, taking universities on their own momentarily (since Lilla gives them the bulk of his attention), that they consist largely of tenured radicals teaching students to nurse identity wounds. To portray universities as having changed from acmes of free thinking into dens of stifling conformity—with humanities faculty modeling the role of thought police for woke students—concedes far too much to a toxic contemporary meme. Even were Lilla's depiction of campus to ring true, he would have to establish how it is a significant player in the fate of the Democratic Party today. No real evidence for this proposition is presented. Lilla tells liberals to get out of their silos, but his prime mover is only the university he knows—and its honestly not clear even how much he knows it, as opposed to what Fox News says about it.

As a result of his obsession with campus, Lilla's long-run 1968-to-narcissism narrative homogenizes too many phenomena that do not fit together well enough. In part, I think this is because Lilla does not really work out how, from individualist self-concern, the common identification with subordinated groups that he calls "identity politics" flows. The fracture of "we" into "me" that he portrays is difficult to see arresting in a series of subgroups, especially when the ones Lilla indicts are communities of sentiment focused on the fate of a set of stigmatized victims—including affiliates and supporters not actually part of those groups. Even if he does have an abstract solution to the individualist foundations of the politics of the subordinated, "finding oneself" as a form of inward-turned political Romanticism is hardly a serious read of many of the group identifications that Lilla wants to include under his heading. It describes a few causes—but not many, let alone most.

Take Lilla's notorious attack on Black Lives Matter. Mainly, Lilla critiques the movement for providing fodder to Fox News and thus devastating the movement's own cause. It is a debatable critique even as a strategic matter. "In democratic politics," Lilla counsels, "it is suicidal to set the bar for agreement higher than necessary for winning adherents and elections." But no successful social movement has ever worked by figuring out in advance how much rectification of injustice society at large will tolerate—and then demanding only exactly that much. A figure such as Martin Luther King, Jr., by no means conceived of himself as the leader of a group defined in advance with claims tailored to what a white majority would accept. Instead, he bet on the creation of a new constituency across racial lines to be brought about in an unpredictable concatenation of imagination and interest.

But more tellingly, Black Lives Matter does not fit in the least with Lilla's larger theory of U.S. narcissism in the first place. Did Black Lives Matter originate when ageing hippies impressed on students an indulgent pseudo-politics of personal authenticity? Hardly. It was a response to the impunity of police, and the liberal choice to collude with conservatives in building a carceral state for the urban black poor rather than reinventing what Lilla praises as Franklin Roosevelt's dispensation to serve them. In short, not neo-Romanticism, but neoconservatism and neoliberalism, were the catalysts for movements such as Black Lives Matter.

The fact is that there has always been a politics of groups in the United States; not much in this regard has changed recently, and you simply do not get very far by linking recently prominent groups to the culture of narcissism, real as it certainly is in our time. Now, it is plausible to say that group campaigns have always articulated some causes rather than others, and articulated them in ways adapted to and shaped by powerful forces in their time. But you might get much further by claiming that, rather than the rise and fall of groups being determined by existential neediness, the victory of economic libertarianism made movements such as trade unions collapse while others were forced into compatibility with the explosion of inequality in our times: racial justice on condition it is class-free, "lean in" neoliberal feminism, and so forth. And to that extent, it is again not a critique of identity politics in the universities that U.S. liberalism needs, but a critique of libertarian economics in society.

All told, the problem in the United States may well have been what Lilla calls "ambient libertarianism," but the flower children are far less to blame for its consequences than the free market ideology of the whole spectrum of American politics for most of modern times—the real force that laid Roosevelt's liberalism low, foiling its extension, no thanks to an assist from early neoconservatives.

BUT IF LILLA'S APPEAL to structural realities in *The Once and Future Liberal* plays far too little a role in his diagnosis, it goes unaccountably missing in his cure, which is a form of civic nationalism. It is the height of ironies: Lilla cuts off his most promising argument after introducing it, using it to explain the identity politics of professors and students before calling for an empty version of nationalism—an identity politics of his own.

Lilla is right to insist that Democrats need a program but wrong to fall silent when it comes to structural justice. Lilla's most persuasive claims come to grief for this reason. He insists that politics is not just about criticizing power, but about exercising it, and therefore winning it. He demands that progressives seek to reconnect with all Americans in every place when they seek not only to mobilize but also to win (though there is no reason to portray a false choice or zero-sum game, as Lilla sometimes does, between mobilizing and winning). And he plausibly contends that, even today, the primary threat Trump presents to his progressive enemies is not "tyranny," but rather that he will tempt them into repeating the mistake of abdicating from offering a major alternative. Resistance, however noble, is not enough, and a new vision for the Democratic Party—or, if it is irredeemable, some new progressive party—is required.

But what new vision? Lilla ends with a kind of void; by his own admission, the civic nationalism with which he concludes is empty. And if he doesn't provide it content, Lilla commits the very same error of failing to empathize with the real interests of white male voters that he indicts in others.

Lilla tells a parable of a fisherman who goes to the water only to scold the fish about their historical sins, as if you do not need bait to hook them—a story he wants to illustrate to spokespeople for oppressed groups that they should soft-pedal their indictments of white supremacy for strategic purposes, so long as white males are needed for Democrats to win elections. Lilla's parable suggests he thinks that the sole alternative to losing red voters is to trick them into voting for blue. But wouldn't it be better to come up with a message that actually registered and reimagined common interests across existing lines?

Without a program, Lilla's summoning of civics in his book is thus merely a communitarian appeal for an *identity party* or an *identity society*—as if he actually agrees with his chosen foes that what people want most (or will work best) is a politics of meaning. Did Lilla come to bury *identity politics*—or simply to praise it at the level of the country? He indicts a politics of symbolism, then finishes by offering one of his own. He castigates a kind of political existentialism, but what else is civic nationalism by itself, if it does not take shape around a new set of policies?

STILL IN SHOCK after Trump's election, U.S. liberals are only beginning to devise a real program for structural justice in the country. The disturbing fact is that, to date, the Democratic Party has mainly avoided the task. To confront it directly would be an unprecedented chance not merely to do good for the country, but to do well for the party's long-term electoral prospects. The true significance of Lilla's intervention, for all the brouhaha it has caused, is as a sign of the discombobulation of liberals who intuit the need to change their ways before they actually move to do so.

For sure, the neo-Rooseveltian dispensation that Lilla calls for is a nonstarter without a contemporary New Deal. It would have to attend to the sort of class justice the original New Deal initiated, including the furtherance of now-longstanding liberal impulses for race and gender justice, while making sure neither looks like a concession to optics in an age of the victory of the rich.

Roosevelt's genius was not to transcend specific identities in the name of U.S. identity, but to insist that markets serve more than the rich.

The fact that this original liberalism did not serve all groups, as Lilla too occasionally concedes, has been an excellent reason for rectifying omissions, which is what many Democrats were trying to do until they were stopped in their tracks after 1968 and the country went another way. Not the New Deal, but that later crossroads, when neoconservatism and neoliberalism arrived, is a good starting point today in our search for a social justice, and therefore a liberalism, the likes of which the United States has yet to see.

Exceptional Victims

Christian G. Appy

EXACTLY A YEAR before he was murdered, Martin Luther King, Jr., gave one of the greatest speeches of his life, a piercing critique of the war in Vietnam. Two thousand people jammed into New York's Riverside Church on April 4, 1967, to hear King shred the historical, political, and moral claims that U.S. leaders had invoked since the end of World War II to justify their counterrevolutionary foreign policy. The United States had not supported Vietnamese independence and democracy, King argued, but had repeatedly opposed it; the United States had not defended the people of South Vietnam from external communist aggression, but was itself the foreign aggressor—burning and bombing villages, forcing peasants off their ancestral land, and killing, by then, as many as one million Vietnamese. "We are on the side of the wealthy, and the secure," King said, "while we create a hell for the poor."

The war was an "enemy of the poor" at home as well. Not only were poor black and white boys sent "to kill and die together for a nation that has been unable to seat them together in the same schools," but the vast expense required to obliterate an impoverished, nonwhite nation 8,000 miles away eviscerated the domestic social programs that had promised to narrow economic and racial inequalities at home. The military draft, for instance, offered deferments and exemptions that favored the privileged while programs such as Project 100,000 enlisted men from "the subterranean poor"—men so badly educated they would once have been rejected for military service. Project 100,000 was touted as a program of social uplift, but in reality, it sent poor men to the front lines as cannon fodder, further proving King's point that the promises of the Great Society were "shot down on the battlefield of Vietnam."

The Riverside Church speech alone should place King in the pantheon of 1960s antiwar activists. Yet in public memory, his opposition to the Vietnam War is largely forgotten. Why? Part of the answer goes back to the media's vitriolic denunciation of the 1967 speech. In a characteristic condemnation, *Life* insisted that King had gone "beyond his personal right to dissent" by advocating "abject surrender" in a "slander that sounded like a script for Radio Hanoi." Many commentators said King should stick to domestic civil rights and let his criticism of U.S. policy stop at the water's edge.

King did not back down. Later that month, he renewed his attacks on the war. "Oh, the press was so noble in its applause . . . when I was saying, 'Be non-violent toward Bull Connor,'" referring to the commissioner of public safety in Birmingham, Alabama, who turned fire hoses and attack dogs on peaceful civil rights demonstrators. But that same press, King continued, "will curse you and damn you when you say, 'Be non-violent toward the little brown Vietnamese children.'"

FIFTY YEARS LATER, we are still plagued by the racial hypocrisy and violence that King denounced. Powerful people and institutions still tolerate and promote racism at home while waging war against nonwhites abroad. Think only of the many police officers who have been acquitted of murdering unarmed African Americans such as Eric Garner and Michael Brown, or of President Donald Trump's insistence that the white supremacists who attacked peaceful counter-protesters in Charlottesville, Virginia, included "some very fine people." Abroad, the Trump administration continues to "bomb the shit out of" foreign targets not just in Afghanistan, Iraq, and Syria, but in Yemen (in league with Saudi Arabia) and in Somalia. Indeed, the U.S. imperial footprint and assertion of military power is nowhere in decline. Since 2013, according to journalist Nick Turse, the United States has conducted military operations in at least 130 countries *every* year, roughly 70 percent of the nations on Earth.

Recent state-sanctioned violence has not gone uncontested. At home there are movements such as Black Lives Matter, and in foreign policy, polls show that since 2006 a majority of Americans have opposed the endless wars in Afghanistan and Iraq. But despite broad antiwar opinion, we do not have a broad and vibrant antiwar culture or movement. That is one of the most striking differences between our own time and the Vietnam era.

The Vietnam War, as I have argued in *American Reckoning: The Vietnam War and Our National Identity* (2015), undermined public faith in U.S. exceptionalism like no other event in our history. Never before had such a wide range of citizens, cutting across lines of class, race, gender, and religion, reject the claim that the United States was a unique and invincible force for good. As King made clear, the Vietnam War blatantly contradicted every assumption of moral superiority, and even prowar hawks were left to wonder how the greatest military power in world history had been unable to prevail against a nation of rice farmers.

To understand our current political moment, we must understand how political and media forces, especially on the right, responded to this embarrassment and to criticisms such as King's. Conservatives at the time were determined to rebuild everything they thought the war had destroyed—U.S. power, pride, prestige, and patriotism. Above all, they sought to resuscitate a faith in U.S. exceptionalism. That restoration project was surprisingly successful, but it produced a new, makeshift form of U.S. exceptionalism that is different from its original model. In place of the universalistic, idealistic, intrinsically confident faith in national superiority of the 1950s, the post-Vietnam version of exceptionalism is ever more nationalistic, defensive, bombastic, and xenophobic. Both versions are dangerously imperialistic and aggressive, but our latest model is more explicitly founded on a demonization of foreign—primarily nonwhite—others.

Perhaps the most characteristic feature of the new U.S. exceptionalism is the belief that the world's greatest nation is not the envy of the world, not a shining city on a hill, but the victim of outrageous and inexplicable attacks from nonwhite countries and cultures. Whether the attacks are real (such as 9/11) or imagined (such as Iraq's weapons of mass destruction), they are almost always attributed to "rogue" nations, terrorist groups, religious extremists, or nonwhite immigrants whose actions are represented as barbaric hate crimes with no plausible historical motive or U.S. provocation.

The new U.S. exceptionalism has many sources but two important ones were born from the bitter memory of failure and defeat in Vietnam: the effective campaigns to vilify the antiwar movement and to instill deference to the military by constructing an image of U.S. troops and veterans as icons of heroic victimhood. These two efforts were mutually reinforcing. Antiwar activists since the Vietnam War have been cast as cowardly draft-dodgers who scorned and betrayed their patriotic peers who served in Vietnam.

Indeed, King is not included in the pantheon of antiwar activists precisely because, in U.S. public life and memory, *there is no peace pantheon* to join. We have no national sites and stories that commemorate the 1960s antiwar movement—no museums, memorials, parks, highways, or holidays. Nowhere can you find a major public celebration of the most diverse and dynamic antiwar movement in U.S. history.

PERHAPS YOU EXPECTED to find it, at long last, in the ten-part, eighteen-hour PBS documentary *The Vietnam War*, by Ken Burns and Lynn Novick. If so, you were disappointed. The 30 million dollar film, released in 2017, features some flattering profiles of Vietnam veterans who joined the antiwar movement, but peace activists who lack a military credential are virtually invisible. The two civilian antiwar activists who do appear (out of eighty interviews) criticize the peace movement more than the war. One of them tearfully apologizes for calling veterans "baby-killers and worse." The film thus reinforces a longstanding myth that the ill-treatment of veterans (for which the government and corporations warrant most of the blame) was perpetrated primarily by the very movement that worked to bring them home.

With veterans so firmly cast as victims of peaceniks in our national consciousness, the next logical step was to offer them automatic hero status. Since 9/11, the ritualized support for troops and veterans, far more symbolic than substantive, has become obsessive. We are encouraged to express our gratitude through yellow ribbons and the mantra of "Thank you for your service," but such demonstrations serve to inhibit national debate about why our government continues to order troops to fight unpopular wars that don't enhance the safety or freedom of anyone.

Moreover, our ritual deference to the military also prevents the common understanding of a basic truth: no large group is heroic by definition. War breeds violence and brutalization, and it is therefore remarkable that the majority of veterans re-enter civilian life peacefully. But not all do. As Kathleen Belew documents in her forthcoming book, *Bring the War Home: The White Power Movement and Paramilitary America*, veterans from Vietnam and every war since have played a significant role in the growth of white supremacist groups. A 2009 report by the Department of Homeland Security, cited by Belew, concluded that the single factor correlating most highly with surges in Ku Klux Klan membership (going all the way back to the 1860s) is an influx of veterans returning from war.

Perhaps it shouldn't be surprising, however, that some Vietnam veterans have found common cause with white supremacists. White supremacists, after all, ascribe to a certain victim status that resonates with the narrative of nationalist victimhood that originated during the Vietnam War itself. By 1972 President Richard Nixon often spoke as if the only reason to continue fighting in Vietnam was to get back our prisoners of war. Never mind that belligerents routinely detain POWs until the war's end; Nixon accused Hanoi of making "barbaric use of our prisoners as negotiating pawns." Nixon's charge set the stage for the greatest of post-Vietnam myths: that the victorious communists of Vietnam continued to hold an unknown number U.S. POWs long after the end of the war.

Hollywood films fueled this fire, perfectly reflecting the culture of xenophobic victimhood. In films such as *Uncommon Valor* (1983), *Missing in Action* (1984), and *Rambo: First Blood Part II* (1985), veterans return to Vietnam to rescue emaciated white comrades, slaughtering hundreds of savage Asians in the process. These fantasies of revenge and national redemption did not depend on evidence or logic. The fact that Vietnam always denied holding postwar POWs and had no apparent motive to do so was taken as further evidence of the former enemy's perfidy. By the early 1990s, roughly two-thirds of Americans believed the charge despite two congressional investigations that failed to discover any persuasive evidence.

Of course, not all foreign assaults were imaginary. The Iran hostage crisis of 1979–81 generated the first major manifestation of national victimhood. While fifty-two U.S. diplomats, marine guards, and CIA agents were held captive, media coverage made it seem as if the entire nation was under assault. Indeed, the ABC show that became *Nightline* was first called *America Held Hostage*. Little effort was made to explain the deep roots of Iranian opposition to U.S. foreign policy that began with the 1953 CIA-orchestrated overthrow of the popular Iranian prime minister Mohammad Mossadegh, and was followed by twenty-six years of support for the brutally repressive Shah of Iran. The hostage-taking was blowback against a long history of U.S. policy, not an inexplicable act of indiscriminate evil.

As the days of captivity ticked by, obsessively counted by the media, President Jimmy Carter launched a rescue operation that had to be aborted when three helicopters malfunctioned in the desert south of Tehran, leaving behind eight dead U.S. crewmen. The failed rescue—"the debacle in the desert," *Time* dubbed it—punctuated a key, if unintended, ingredient of victim culture: a sense of helplessness to achieve complete and unambiguous retribution against the nation's tormentors.

The ghost of defeat in Vietnam continues to haunt the stewards of the U.S. empire as it lurches further into its decline. Over the past fifty years, no "victory" has been perceived as permanent or significant enough. At the end of the 1991 Persian Gulf War, when President George W. H. Bush claimed that "the specter of Vietnam has been buried forever in the desert sands of the Arabian Peninsula," he did not realize how short-lived that victory would be. Indeed, as Trump lamented when announcing his candidacy for president, "We don't have victories anymore."

IN ITS HEYDAY, U.S. exceptionalism relied on the "absolute victory" and "inevitable triumph" promised by President Franklin Roosevelt on the day after Pearl Harbor in 1941. It underwrote President John F. Kennedy's famous vow that the United States "shall pay any price, bear any burden, meet any hardship, support any friend, oppose any foe to assure the survival and the success of liberty." But, by contrast, the version of exceptionalism cobbled together out of the tatters of the Vietnam era can make no such promises. Nationalism today is founded more on grievance than confidence, more on belligerent victimhood than idealistic messianism.

Since 9/11 and President George W. Bush's declaration of a Global War on Terror, xenophobic Americanism has come into full flower. As Bush put it ten days after 9/11, "Every nation, in every region, now has a decision to make: either you are with us, or you are with the terrorists." The "terrorists," it turned out, were almost always racialized as nonwhite, while white domestic terrorists such as Timothy McVeigh (who killed 168 people in Oklahoma City in 1995) have been cast as criminals or madmen.

By every measure, Bush's Global War on Terror, as well as its iterations under Barack Obama and Trump, have been colossal failures. And the parallels between U.S. policies in Vietnam and in our twenty-first century wars are staggering. In all three theaters, we have seen undeclared wars waged under false pretexts, and we have deployed hundreds of thousands of U.S. troops to lands where they were widely perceived as hostile invaders. The mission has been to prop up foreign governments that cannot gain the broad support of their own people, and we have fought brutal counterinsurgencies guaranteed to maim, kill, or displace countless civilians. Once again, the fighting has persisted long after a majority of Americans deemed it mistaken or immoral, and once again, the government has failed to achieve its stated objectives.

But for those who preside over the U.S. empire, all that matters is sustaining U.S. power, however illusory or ineffective it may be. Trump is the natural result of the brittle, defensive form of U.S. exceptionalism that originated after Vietnam, and he epitomizes the bellicose nationalism I have been describing. Every day he presents himself as the victim of lies and unjustified attacks. Every day he lashes back with whatever new "reality" he decides to invent. Evidence of success or failure, truth or falsehood, is irrelevant. Each failure is either called a success or used to justify further attacks on perceived enemies at home or abroad. Government policy is now, more than ever, an "enemy of the poor," and we have not addressed the persistent racial injustices that are, as King made clear, inextricably linked to our foreign policy. Trump represents, in absurd extremes, the narcissism, self-delusion, and abdication of responsibility that are part of this country's failure to reckon with the criminality and corrosiveness of its imperial exploits.

King cautioned against this outcome, and he offered—and through his words, continues to offer—another path forward, one of relentless self-criticism and mature self-interrogation meant to inspire a revolution of values and uproot the machinery of imperialism. The Vietnam War, he warned, was "a symptom of a far deeper malady."

Unless there was a "revolution of values," the "giant triplets of racism, extreme materialism, and militarism" would continue to betray the nation's greatest ideals. Meaningful change required not only the end of war in Vietnam, but the replacement of allegiances to "tribe, race, class, and nation" with "loyalty to mankind as a whole." Without these radical transformations, King concluded, the United States would remain "the greatest purveyor of violence in the world."

Part of our failure to attend to this dimension of King's thought is, paradoxically, rooted in his hagiography. Our reflexive genuflection to military service goes hand in hand with our failure to treat antiwar protestors as real heroes of U.S. democracy. King's antiwar critique unsettles something very insidious and essential to the reproduction of empire. Cleaving it off was the price of admission into the U.S. pantheon of heroes.

The Almost Inevitable Failure of Justice

Thad Williamson

IN HIS FINAL BOOK, *Where Do We Go From Here* (1967), Martin Luther King, Jr., warned that the struggle for black equality had moved into a more difficult phase that would test the moral commitments of white America to democracy. King commented that, for most whites, the battles over school desegregation and the Civil Rights Act had merely "been a struggle to treat the Negro with a degree of decency, not of equality":

> White America was ready to demand that the Negro should be spared the
> lash of brutality and coarse degradation, but it had never been truly commit-
> ted to helping him out of poverty, exploitation or all forms of discrimination.

King's warning about the thinness of the country's commitment to democracy was combined with a profound optimism that ending poverty and creating a truly free society was within reach—that Americans might at last choose justice. His optimism was consonant with and informed by social and policy analysis of the time. Three years earlier, the Johnson administration had launched its War on Poverty, and in *Where Do We Go From Here*, King quoted the analysis of Hyman Bookbinder—from President Lyndon B. Johnson's Office of Economic Opportunity—that "the poor can stop being poor if the rich are willing to become even richer at a slower rate."

Twenty years later, when William Julius Wilson published *The Truly Disadvantaged*, his landmark assessment of the causes and consequences of ghetto poverty, it may have still been possible to view inner-city poverty as simply unfinished business from the civil rights movement. After all, African Americans had made substantial economic gains since the 1960s, and Ronald Reagan's presidency could be seen as an aberration, the last vestige of reaction against inevitable social change. In his successful 1988 run for the presidency, Reagan's vice president, George H. W. Bush, even allowed that he was haunted by the fate of ghetto children.

But today, after another thirty years, it is hard not to fear that the persistence of racial injustice and U.S. poverty is anything but a permanent feature of our democracy. There have been pilot and demonstration programs, tax incentives, competitive grant initiatives, and other policy steps aimed at steering investment toward low-income communities. Indeed, the initiatives of the Clinton administration—such as the Community Development Financial Institutions Fund, HOPE VI, New Market Tax Credits, and Moving to Opportunity—were followed by Promise Zones, Promise Neighborhoods, and Choice Neighborhoods in the Obama administration. Especially under Obama, federal programs sought to induce localities to engage in comprehensive planning, adopt best practices, and provide holistic support to neighborhoods and families involved in or impacted by community redevelopment efforts.

These initiatives generally had decent intentions, but their most notable quality is their sheer modesty relative to need. None of them, alone or together, represent the kind of massive assault on urban poverty briefly championed by the Office of Economic Opportunity in the 1960s. The federal government continues to spend much more money supporting suburban homeowners through the mortgage interest tax deduction than it does programs aimed at "transforming" urban communities.

Most tellingly, not even Democratic administrations have set tangible goals for reducing poverty nationwide. Rather than imagine full-scale national initiatives (such as the massive job program that some within Johnson's administration wanted at the heart of the War on Poverty), liberal social policy has, at its best, been content with relatively marginal change in a limited number of communities. At worst, it has drifted away from concern with what John Rawls termed in 1971 the "background structure" of social justice—our fundamental political and economic institutions—to the decidedly secondary question of the behavior and activities of the poor themselves. Clinton's 1996 welfare reform law, for example, featured a framework far more oriented toward coercion and sanctions than crafting effective pathways to prosperity.

Despite near-universal handwringing over the persistence of ghetto poverty over the past three decades, official national policy has been de facto fatalism. This is not just a policy failure. In Rawlsian terms, it is a failure of basic justice because it is a failure of shared moral commitments to liberty, equality, and respect for the inherent dignity of all persons.

PHILOSOPHER TOMMIE SHELBY, author of *Dark Ghettos: Injustice, Dissent, and Reform* (2017), uses a Rawlsian framework to challenge the dominant understanding of the "ghetto" and its residents. In keeping with the tradition of critique by African American social scientists from Horace R. Cayton, Jr., and St. Clair Drake to Kenneth and Mamie Clark, Shelby uses the term "ghetto" to refer to "black, high poverty metropolitan neighborhoods" that suffer "from a relative lack of nearby or readily accessible goods, services, and opportunities that are needed

Williamson

for human flourishing." His book tackles some of the thorniest issues in urban social policy—residential integration, the so-called "culture of poverty," reproduction, family, joblessness, crime and punishment, and cultural expressions of dissent—from a principled egalitarian position. He is consistently informed by a determination to show respect for inner-city residents and their actual and potential agency as equal citizens.

The result is instructive and pathbreaking in three key respects. First, Shelby considers the moral implications of U.S. society's failure to provide basic justice to a significant portion of its citizens. To what extent and under what circumstances, then is it reasonable to ask such citizens to comply with state policies that reflect injustice?

Second, Shelby takes up the more ambitious task of developing an account of "corrective justice"—how the failure to provide basic justice can be rectified—and a corresponding account of "political ethics," or the "principles and values that should guide individuals as they respond to social injustices."

Third, Shelby calls for renewed attention to the centrality of race in understanding the U.S. failure to provide basic justice. The reluctance of many white Americans to view persons of color as fully equal citizens, entitled to basic social and economic rights and opportunities, has led to the presumption, embedded in the design and implementation of safety-net policies, that there is something inherently wrong or deficient with the behavior of poor persons, especially poor persons of color.

Shelby's assessment of the U.S. welfare state and the persistence of ghetto poverty thus runs as follows: as a matter of justice, all Americans are entitled to substantially equal opportunities. At a minimum, this includes decent material background conditions combined with a guarantee of a basic income or equivalent device, but it also includes what Rawls termed "fair equality of opportunity," namely that access to life-shaping opportunities should not be contingent on the socioeconomic status of one's parents.

The very existence and persistence of the urban ghetto, however, shows that the United States does not provide this background justice. In fact, the social policies it employs largely fail to show respect for low-income Americans, especially low-income African Americans. Instead, they are often paternalistic, requiring recipients to adhere to certain socially acceptable behaviors in order to access benefits. Some programs go even further and aim at the "cultural reform" of their participants and the inner city itself.

Shelby argues that ghetto residents are well within their rights when they refuse to comply with such paternalistic policies. In a just society, access to basic needs such as housing and food should not be contingent on compliance with mainstream behavioral norms. Indeed, defiance of mainstream values is often, Shelby believes, a legitimate (if often mis-recognized) expression of protest against injustice. Shelby's hope is that such protest, following some promising early steps made by Black Lives Matter, will coalesce into a tangible political force that calls attention to the injustice of current social arrangements.

Importantly, Shelby makes a distinction between the "medical model" of assessing poverty and economic disadvantage and what he terms the "systemic-injustice" model. Most policy discourse sees the "background structure" of society as given and then looks for efficient ways to treat social ills such as unemployment. A systemic-injustice perspective, in contrast, scrutinizes the core institutional factors that shape the distribution of opportunities: the distribution of wealth, the organization of the economy and labor market, the organization of public education and of local government, and conceivably much else as well.

Shelby might have added that "medical model" policy prescriptions are often doomed to fail because isolated policy improvements will almost never overcome deeply flawed structural arrangements. And he might have usefully extended the argument in two directions.

First, Shelby's critique of ghetto poverty stops short of a reckoning with the failures of welfare-state capitalism itself. The lopsided distribution of wealth characteristic of U.S. capitalism must be on the table in any discussion about realizing social justice—including the discussion of ghetto poverty. Rawls himself argued that welfare-state capitalism is incompatible with justice, partly because it never realizes its own stated aspirations and partly because its reliance on post-tax redistribution creates a debilitating, unstable dynamic of mutual resentment between more and less prosperous citizens. (See *Property-Owning Democracy: Rawls and Beyond*, edited by Martin O'Neill and Thad Williamson, for extended discussion). In other words, a politics that aims to create a just background structure needs to have a clear, positive account of the basic institutional configurations of a just political economy. The economic policy program released by the Movement for Black Lives is an impressive initial effort to begin mapping that background structure.

Second, Shelby doesn't ask whether, in the absence of a mass movement capable of putting fundamental issues on the table, policymakers can overcome political resistance to addressing structural injustice. After all, partisan and resource constraints almost inevitably lead even the best-intentioned policymakers back to some version of the medical model.

ALMOST INEVITABLY. But not literally inevitably. Consider Richmond, Virginia, which has an overall poverty rate of 25 percent and a child poverty rate of approximately 40 percent. From the formation of the Mayor's Anti-Poverty Commission under former mayor Dwight C. Jones, to the launch and development of the Office of Community Wealth Building (OCWB), a city agency charged with moving thousands of residents out of poverty in the coming decade, the city has drawn attention for its efforts to fight poverty.

Full disclosure: I am not an impartial observer. I served on the Mayor's Anti-Poverty Commission, chaired one of its task forces, and was lead author of its final report. In 2014 I began a two-year term as the first director of the Office of Community Wealth Building while on leave from the University of Richmond. I now serve part-time as a senior policy advisor for current mayor Levar M. Stoney, who has championed expanding the effort.

OCWB does three things that are relatively unique in the policy world. First, it openly embraces a structural understanding of concentrated poverty in Richmond. The commission's report documents the historical factors—such as redlining, resistance to school integration, and white flight—that produced neighborhoods in which the average income is less than 10,000 dollars a year and nearly 100 percent of residents are persons of color. Likewise, its policy recommendations focus squarely on those structural factors that reproduce poverty: underemployment, substandard public education, substandard provision of public housing, and substandard provision (or nonexistence) of public transportation. This orientation was by design. As lead author of the commission's report, I (like several colleagues in the effort) was determined to keep the focus on structural underemployment and related factors rather than on the behaviors or "culture" of residents living in poverty.

Second, OCWB and the City of Richmond have set ambitious policy targets: cutting overall poverty 40 percent by the year 2030 and child poverty 50 percent by the same year. This entails moving 1,000 *additional* people a year out of poverty relative to the status quo and maintaining that movement each year for a decade. The aspiration is to create a virtuous circle in which more local residents working and earning good money strengthens the city tax base, more stable families help strengthen school performance for the city's children, and more resources are available to reinvest in ongoing needs. Achieving this level of change will require not just one or two new programs, but scrutiny and change in multiple policy arenas, at multiple levels of government.

Third, OCWB has made a good-faith effort to engage people in poverty as partners. The Maggie L. Walker Citizens Advisory Board (CAB) gives low-income residents a voice in the design and implementation process of the various workforce, educational, housing, and transportation initiatives led or championed by the office. In 2014 the Richmond City Council codified the CAB as a permanent advisory body, and by law, over half of its members must reside in high-poverty neighborhoods. Thus the initiative aims to build community wealth in the very neighborhoods that have been historically underinvested in and to transform communities of concentrated poverty through a people-centered process.

Surprisingly perhaps given the existing political climate, this explicitly structural approach—which is informed by the same kinds of concerns that animate Shelby's work—has gained traction in a city whose entire history has been defined by systemic, race-based inequity and by efforts to resist and overcome injustices. The very boldness of the charge has helped build significant support. In spring of 2017, the Commonwealth of Virginia set aside 7.5 million dollars to support local-ities undertaking community wealth building initiatives with matching grants; the City of Richmond received nearly 2 million dollars of this funding from the Virginia Department of Social Services, allowing for a substantial expansion of its workforce development program in the current fiscal year. The work of OCWB has also received significant interest and recognition from national publications and organizations.

But as OCWB engages the substance of its work—helping connect underemployed residents to living-wage jobs—practical challenges blur the distinction between the medical model and the structural approach. For instance, to access the supplementary resources OCWB offers (such as training, transportation, and child care), a low-income resident must commit to seeking employment. This requirement is essential to its political viability but is also, I would argue, morally defensible given the scarcity of resources. Richmond does not have sufficient funds to provide all residents a basic income, nor would there be political support for such an approach.

On the ground, seeking structural justice in a deeply flawed regime inevitably involves a practical reconciliation—if not moral compromise—with those aspects of the social structure that policymakers cannot realistically impact. Success in this context often involves wise discernment and then aggressive action on those things that are within policymakers' sphere of influence.

SO WHAT IS the endgame?

We may need not one but two modes of political ethics for addressing ghetto poverty. The first is exactly what Shelby proposes: more and more citizens calling for bold structural change and building political support for significant redistribution and reallocation of resources. The second, less explored, is an ethic for policymakers trying to advance structural change within the messy terrain of existing local democratic politics. This might mean being able to express a structural approach in terms that adherents to a medical model will understand. And it might mean adhering to some of the same norms (such as evaluations or cost–benefit analyses) from that model that are a precondition of maintaining political and financial support. Intellectual clarity is a great virtue in that context, but ideological purity generally is not.

If there were already a strong consensus and social commitment to Rawlsian-style liberal egalitarianism, Shelby's call for the abolition of ghetto poverty would not be necessary. Quite evidently, such a consensus is lacking. The persistence of the ghetto and the rise of Trumpism reinforce the notion that society can be usefully divided into "these people" and "those people." It is these very divisions, which are antithetical to the strong sense of solidarity a Rawlsian regime requires, that Trumpist politics seeks to exploit, highlight, and perpetuate.

A robust answer to Trumpism will thus require building a broader and bolder political coalition capable of both naming and addressing structural injustices. Shelby's powerful analysis must be brought into dialogue with other recent work focused on the discontent of the "white working class," victims of economic displacement, and the working class more generally outside of the urban ghetto.

It will also require a decidedly bolder flavor of progressive politics at the national level. While the Richmond example shows the potential of local efforts in addressing core structural justice, it is the larger-order national policies that set the context in which localities must operate. With a bundle of bold strategies, the federal government must play the lead role in any effort truly designed to replace the ghetto with a more just distribution of resources and opportunities. Shelby leaves those strategies to others. But policymakers and politicians should take his moral message of abolitionism to heart. To fail to do so is to acquiesce to the persistence of deep injustice—economic and racial—for yet another generation.

THE QUESTION for us is the same as it was for King fifty years ago: "Where do we go from here?" King believed that poverty could be abolished in a reasonably fast period of time, with an expenditure of resources and effort that would be significant, even costly, yet well within the nation's capacity.

The missing ingredient now, as then, is sufficient political will and imagination. "There is nothing but a lack of social vision to prevent us from paying an adequate wage to every American citizen whether he be a hospital worker, laundry worker, maid or day laborer," King wrote in *Where Do We Go From Here*. "There is nothing except shortsightedness to prevent us from guaranteeing an annual minimum—and *livable*—income for every American family."

As King knew, pilot projects and small adjustments do not address systemic injustice or suffice to combat centuries of accumulated injustice. What is required is a resource and policy commitment commensurate with the scale of the issues being addressed, combined with the ethical and political determination to remold "a recalcitrant status quo with bruised hands until we have fashioned it into a brotherhood."

Christian G. Appy is Professor of History at the University of Massachusetts Amherst and author of *American Reckoning: The Vietnam War and Our National Identity*.

Andrew Douglas, author of *In the Spirit of Critique: Thinking Politically in the Dialectical Tradition*, is Associate Professor of Political Science at Morehouse College.

Bernard E. Harcourt is the Isidor and Seville Sulzbacher Professor of Law and Professor of Political Science at Columbia University. His book *The Counterrevolution: How Our Government Went to War Against Its Own Citizens* is forthcoming.

Elizabeth Hinton is Assistant Professor of History and of African and African American Studies at Harvard University. Her book *From the War on Poverty to the War on Crime: The Making of Mass Incarceration in America*, was a *New York Times* 2016 notable book.

Samuel Moyn is Professor of Law and History at Yale University. His latest book is *Not Enough: Human Rights in an Unequal World*.

Ed Pavlić, Distinguished Research Professor of English and African American Studies at the University of Georgia, is a scholar, poet, and novelist. He is author of *Who Can Afford to Improvise?: James Baldwin and Black Music, the Lyric and the Listeners*.

Aziz Rana is Professor of Law at Cornell University and the author of *The Two Faces of American Freedom*.

Barbara Ransby is Professor of History, African-American Studies, and Gender and Women's Studies at the University of Illinois at Chicago. Her book *Making All Black Lives Matter: Reimagining Freedom in the Twenty-First Century* is out this summer.

Keenanga-Yamahtta Taylor, author of the recent *From #BlackLivesMatter to Black Liberation*, is Assistant Professor of African American Studies at Princeton University.

Brandon M. Terry is Assistant Professor of African and African American Studies and Social Studies at Harvard University and coeditor, with Tommie Shelby, of *To Shape a New World: Essays on the Political Philosophy of Martin Luther King, Jr.*

Jeanne Theoharis is Distinguished Professor of Political Science at Brooklyn College and author of *The Rebellious Life of Mrs. Rosa Parks*, which won a 2014 NAACP Image Award.

Thad Williamson is Associate Professor of Leadership Studies and Philosophy, Politics, Economics & Law at the University of Richmond. His books include *Property-Owning Democracy: Rawls and Beyond*, coedited with Martin O'Neill. Views expressed here are his own.